Pirates In The Mists

Pirates and Villains Of The North Carolina Coast

Joe Sledge

Books By Joe Sledge

Did You See That? A Travel Guide To North Carolina's Out Of The Ordinary Attractions

Did You See That? On The Outer Banks

Did You See That? Too!

Did You See That Ghost?

Haunting The Outer Banks

In The Shadows Of The Pines

Haunting The Carolina Coast

Haunting The Cape Fear Coast

Pirates In The Mists

The Unmerciful Sea

(As John Martell)

Bess Truly And Her Zap-Gun Rangers

Republished, as Editor and additional material

Nag's Head; Or, Two Months Among The Bankers

Kinnakeet Adventure

PIRATES IN THE MISTS

PIRATES AND VILLAINS
ACROSS THE NORTH CAROLINA COAST

JOE SLEDGE

For Callie

Table Of Contents

Introduction

North Carolina has a unique love affair with the rogues and rascals that are part of our pirate lore. Blackbeard has become a favorite son of sorts for Ocracoke, Bath, as well as up and down all the other coastal towns and villages. There isn't a gift shop or souvenir store on the entire Atlantic coast that hasn't sold a poster or resin figure of the pirate to admiring fans, whether they be tourist or local.

Now, Blackbeard has had over three hundred years of good press to help promote his popularity. He became a larger than life story, a great and terrifying threat, even within his own lifetime. And even after, his legend continued. It was said that after Lt. Maynard removed Blackbeard's head with a swift slice from his cutlass, the body was dumped overboard, where it proceeded to swim around the ship three times in vain hope of finding his head, just so he could continue the fight. The story went that Blackbeard was so evil that heaven didn't want him and hell was too afraid to let him in.

Now, the reality of piracy back at the turn of the 18th century was much less colorful and popular. A sailor's life was rough, and a pirate's life could be much worse, and incredibly short. Edward Teach, the man behind the legend of Blackbeard, would really only ply the Atlantic for less than two years. It was hardly a dynasty of epic proportions.

1

But, still, we love our pirates. Time has given them a mystery, a mythos, to which we attach ourselves. From the pirate invasion at Beaufort to the old Pirate Jamboree back in the days on the Outer Banks, we love, we *love*, to dress up as those scoundrels, the blackguards, the mischief-makers that we picture pirates as from long ago. They were Robin Hoods, taking from wealthy bloated merchant ships and selling, for a bit of a profit, to the everyman. And they got to cavort around the sunny Caribbean beaches drinking rum and yo-ho-ho-ing, saying "Yarrr!" with a squinty eye on a warm day on the beach. It was the life we all wanted. Not just as kids, but the adults, too. We all wanted to be free, just for a while, to sail where the stars told us. We would have no one to answer to, adventure was around the next island, and monsters and gold lay everywhere on some old crusty map with burned edges.

That's what the legend of pirates brings us here on the coast of North Carolina. It's a wild sense of freedom, an escape from the day to day. That's why we look at pirates, well, at least some of them, or what they represent, as heroes and idols. There are some people who only like to tell the real history, to correct the made up parts of the tales that were written years, decades, or centuries later. The reason we picture Blackbeard as a barrel chested madman saying "Arrr, matey!" is more because of Robert Newton's portrayal of the legendary buccaneer in the 1952 movie *Blackbeard, The Pirate*.

But here's the thing. Sure, we know not everything we say about pirates along our coast is true. We get it, treasure isn't buried just under every little hill or just out of reach below our beach towel. We are not a few feet away from cursed Spanish doubloons.

But isn't it fun to think about it?

It's fun, that's the point. We enjoy this. We want to be pirates, but we want to be the fun, wild, knee on the gunwale, cutlass in our hand, salt wind in our face guy or gal that looks like that cheap resin figure we saw in the gift shop, next to the little box covered with glued on cowrie shells. Stop spoiling a perfectly good bit of pretend with reality. We get enough of that at work.

So here are some great stories about pirates and villains across the North Carolina coast. Some are tales of great adventure and risk, while others are about truly bad people who got their comeuppance. They aren't all the tall rough men in long black cloaks with peglegs and eyepatches and a parrot on the shoulder, no. Some of the history of piracy truly was horrible. Some of it stretches the truth. Some of it's just legend and campfire tales. Again, we know, we know. It's not all true.

But it sure is fun.

Captain Kidd

Pirates are greedy and confident by nature. That came back to haunt one seafaring captain off the coast of North Carolina.

William Kidd had a price on his head.

That will happen when you are a pirate. It was true for most all who chose the career, he knew. But in his case, he may have thought it wasn't entirely his fault.

He certainly was a pirate; he had the paper that said so. He had grown up in the life, sought it out, and he had been rather good at it. Up until everything turned on him.

He was born in Scotland, but quickly immigrated as a young man to New York City, which had only recently been turned over to England from the Dutch after years of bloody battles. In 1689, he had established himself as a seafaring man by sailing with a French and English crew in the Caribbean. He quickly made a name for himself as a pirate by stealing the very ship upon which he sailed during a mutiny. He took the ship and became a privateer, with a colonial charter from an English governor on the Caribbean island of Nevis. With his rights to sail for England, Kidd personally declared war on France, and began his short lived life as a buccaneer.

But what a life it was! He became a popular figure back in his home of New York. Blessed with riches, he spread his wealth around, and gained support from powerful people on both sides of the Atlantic. Richard Coote, who was the Earl of Belmont and the appointed colonial governor of New York, Massachusetts, and New Hampshire, asked Kidd to hunt pirates who were enemies of the colonies, as well as any French ships he may come across. If the blessings of the colonial government weren't enough, Kidd also received a letter of marque from King William III. The letter of marque was a cherished document. It essentially declared that the name on the certificate could be a legal pirate for the nation that notarized it. Kidd now was a privateer, a legal pirate working for Great Britain. As long as he presented ten percent of his prizes to the crown, followed the most basic of rules, and only attacked the enemies of England and the colonies, the letter of marque left him in the clear.

Unfortunately for Kidd, he found a way to break every single rule put forth, all the while having his luck change like the winds in his sails.

In 1896, he was presented with his ship, the *Adventure Galley*, paid for in part by British royalty who supported Kidd, but who also expected a positive return on their investment. Kidd set forth to the Indian Ocean to hunt for the French. He would find only struggles, challenges, defections, and defeat. Kidd would take few prizes, while his crew would leave him for more successful ships. Additionally, while he was able to attack and capture a French and Armenian ship, laden with treasures, it was captained by an

Englishman, which would be one of many events that would come to haunt Captain Kidd.

It didn't help that, at one time, a crew member challenged Kidd to attack a Dutch ship. With his benefactor King William III being Dutch even as he sat on the English throne, and England not being at war with the Dutch, Kidd would not. His crew member, William Moore, was none too happy with the loss of potential booty, saying Kidd had brought ruin to him and the rest of the crew. Angered, Kidd dropped a heavy metal bucket on Moore's head. The strike cracked open the gunner's skull, and Moore would die the next day.

While pirates were known for their piratical activities, killing a crew member was one of the few things that was beyond the pale. It would be yet another action that Kidd would have to answer to.

With his luck running out, and his ships worm ridden and leaking, he went back to the more well known climes of the Caribbean. Kidd had been branded a pirate, and no paper was going to change that. He had hoped to take advantage of a royal pardon, but his name was specifically mentioned as not being allowed to collect on the forgiveness. It was a bad sign for Kidd.

Kidd had still held on to hope that his friends in high places, the governor of New York, the lords that had paid for his ship, even the King of England himself, would bring themselves to back their old friend, especially since they had all signed papers to allow Kidd to become a pirate in the first place.

But just to be sure, Kidd sold all his ill-gotten gains for gold and treasure, and while passing by the calm grassy inner shores of the Carolinas, he decided to plant some insurance in the soft sands. Kidd would look upon the churning mouth of the Cape Fear and the safer islands inland more than forty years before any permanent settlement would grace the land that would later become Wilmington. Isolated, quiet, but with easy access to the water, this would be a perfect place to hide his treasure.

With his remaining skeleton crew, still loyal to the captain, Kidd would bury two chests laden with coins, gold chains, and jewels. Where he buried the chests, he marked with small sapling trees to grow nearby on a low hammock of sand.

He knew the risks of going back to face his charges, for him and his crew. He left one trusted lieutenant, John Redfield, to stand guard over his treasure. Redfield was left with three small chests of gold and silver, along with a sailboat, with orders to protect the chests. Redfield was to take from the smaller chests to provide for himself to build a small shack and to acquire food in trade.

Captain Kidd hoped that his personal contacts in the government would protect or forgive him. Pirates were notorious for their barbarous and violent behavior. Did they really expect anything different from Kidd? Perhaps Kidd's benefactors would supply a nod and a wink of understanding. Kidd had been the one who helped support King William's Trinity Church in New York, hadn't he? He knew in his heart that all charges would quickly be dropped.

But just in case, he planned to use the treasure he had buried to buy his way out of trouble. What his charm and good looks couldn't buy, heaps of gold surely would.

Kidd would find out two years later in London that this would not be the case. His supporters turned against him, not wanting to be associated with a pirate and murderer. Kidd would be tried and found guilty. When he was strung up in front of the throngs of people who had come for the macabre sport of death, the rope broke, and he collapsed to the ground. The bloodthirsty crowd suddenly turned spiritual. When a rope breaks at a hanging, it is a sign of divine innocence. They called for Kidd to be spared a second attempt. But Captain Kidd was too much of an embarrassment to be allowed to live. So a second noose was fashioned, and he was hanged until he was dead, dead, dead.

Then his body was strung up over the River Thames, let to rot for three years, as a warning to others who would attempt a similar career.

Pirates beware.

A pirate's life was often course, perilous, and short. Few, if any, of these brigands ever made it to a ripe old age. William Kidd would be just one of many who would swing on the hangman's noose. His life would be sucked out at he gasped for his last breaths through a scratchy and rough knot of a rope.

William Kidd would die on the executioner's dock on May 23, 1701.

But his legend would only just be beginning.

It would take time for news to travel first to the colonies, and then down to John Redfield's little guardian shack, which he had expanded to a nice home. Redfield traveled to more prosperous coastal settlements, including the newly founded Charleston. Redfield, a skilled sailor, a charming rogue, handsome and wealthy, quickly found a wife to share his home. But fears of others searching for Kidd's treasure and possibly harming her as leverage sent him to more proper climes. He took from his stashes and stores enough gold to set him up in the port town, where he and his wife lived a life of comfort. They ultimately had children and grandchildren, and by that time, he Redfield ready to tell his story.

He shared his tales as life aboard the *Adventure Galley* along with his time as a privateer under Captain Kidd. Ultimately, Redfield spilled his secret to his children about the chests of gold and jewels hidden somewhere along the Carolina marshes to the north. Now an old man, he was content with his life in Charleston, and had no wishes for the wealth hidden under the islands of the coast. He would tell his tales to his real treasure, his progeny and his grandchildren that sat rapt at his tales of life as a pirate.

But kids will be kids, and the lure of gold is strong.

His descendants would find their way to the Cape Fear possibly a hundred years later. The low sandy islands were once inhabited by only shorebirds, unaware of the riches beneath their beaks as they peck for tiny coquinas to eat. By the time the descendants of James Redfield arrived, there would be people living on the lands. It is thought that Redfield left servants or enslaved people, who kept the stories alive as Brunswicktown and later Wilmington grew. By this time, the Redfield clan were hungry for something more substantial than seafood.

Redfield had explained that the two chests left by Kidd had been marked by small trees plucked from the sand and replanted by the pirate. To the untrained eye, they would just be yet another grove of salted dwarf trees or some hardy shrub, but to those in the know, the inside firsthand knowledge, they were better than any X that marked the spot.

Curiously, even though the land was untouched, and no visitor had even thought to explore these empty low islands, no treasure was ever found. The Redfield sires, hot, sandy, overworked, and far from home, decided to return to the guaranteed comfort of the life of a wealthy family in genteel Charleston rather than continue to explore for a treasure that might never be discovered.

But that did not mean that others wouldn't take up the shovel in fair hope of discovering the untold riches of a pirate long dead and gone. In the early 1900s, a pair of men camped on the island during the day, and dug by lantern light late at night. After four nights of digging, they found some silver coins and scraps of gold. It was thought that the men employed two young local boys to dig into the water where they thought the chests were buried. When the kids found scraps of metal and a few coins, the men sent the treasures back with the two boys, then went back for the bulk of the treasure for themselves. At least, that's what the boys told their parents after they went back to the empty, abandoned island.

The treasure may have been found, or may not. It may never have even been there. James Redfield really did serve with Captain Kidd, and did live a long life in Charleston. But it could have been just a tale that an old pirate told to entertain his progeny. Certainly many people began to doubt the story over the decades.

Probably right up until the Intracoastal Waterway was dug. By the 1930s, the Intracoastal was immensely more valuable than any treasure. It would provide a safe inner passage for ships and barges to pass across the coast of North Carolina, while avoiding the treacherous Graveyard of the Atlantic and the churning ocean waters that took so many ships to their watery graves.

In 1934, the last of the Intracoastal Waterway was cut from the Cape Fear all the way to the South Carolina border. In the way was the now well named Money Island, the legendary home of Kidd's treasure. By now, if people believed there ever was a treasure, most believed it was under water as the island shifted, or torn to bits by the slow relentless fingers of the tree roots that had once marked the location of the treasure chests. Even the trees themselves were long gone. The salt air, the brackish water, the perpetual waves from boats and winds from storms that had washed over the island had done their dirty work of killing off whatever trees may have ever taken root there.

The damage of storms and swells were nothing in comparison to what the dredges of the U.S. Army Corps of

Engineers could do. Money Island was in the way, and that just couldn't be allowed. The island was dredged and cut in two, with the middle removed for deep passage of the ships carrying seafood, fertilizer, wood, and ultimately pleasure craft. The sand was dredged up and cast aside, the unwanted spoil of an island in the way.

But when the island was dredged, in with the sand and mud came gold chains, coins, and bits of a metal frame from a chest. Perhaps what no descendant of James Redfield could find, what no treasure seeker was able to dig up, the incessant destruction of an engineer's dredge intake was finally able to discover.

However, no more treasure ever came up from Money Island.

So Money Island sits low in the water, merely a legend, with little value outside of framing a sunset. Not that it was ever worthless. And even that small value would mean that it would ultimately end up under someone's ownership.

James Sprunt was wealthy beyond measure. He made his fortune in exporting local cotton to England and the European continent. His excessive wealth let him not only become excessively benevolent with his money, but also to purchase Orton Plantation as a gift to his wife, to move out of his home in the city, the former Governor Dudley mansion. In addition to the sprawling plantation on the river, he acquired, among other pieces of land, Money Island.

While Sprunt had wealth to spare in the form of material riches, his friends and family were even more valuable. And one close friend had his own version of wealth, a dedicated benevolence to treating diseases in far off countries. Dr. George Worth was from Wilmington, though his home was more often in China. It was long, demanding work, and after five years at his task, he had to come home to rest.

Dr. Worth knew there was no treasure on Money Island. He had lived in Wilmington long enough to both know the legend and to know that nothing had been found in all the time since Kidd had passed through.

That didn't stop him from "discovering" a long lost treasure map to Kidd's hidden fortune.

He would come to the Sprunt home, full of tales from his travels, and ultimately he would unfurl the dusty, torn, and burned map onto the dining table, for all to see, especially the young Sprunt children, the nieces and nephews, and the offspring of close friends. Marked with strange symbols, he would read off the old script written in inky black. It would describe the location of Kidd's treasure, guarded by the ghosts of pirates from long ago, and only accessible during a full moon. Good fortune shined like moonlight in that there was a full moon coming the next night, so they must prepare.

Worth would lead the children over in a boat, with the families beside them, all carrying lanterns to light the passage. The older children would be conspicuously absent from the journey. The group of kids and adults would arrive at dark, just in time to see the moon rise over the barrier islands to the east.

In the distance, strange sounds would ring out from the bushes and sea oats. Possibly the ghosts of Kidd and his crew, perhaps only birds disturbed from their nocturnal rest. They must hurry, but be quiet, too. Don't disturb the pirates as they eternally rest on this one night.

On an open little hillock, a small mound of silty sand, the children discover their treasure, just where the map had promised. Crystals, jewels and jewelry, as well as coins from far distant countries, all with strange indecipherable markings. They would collect their indescribable booty, its value incalculable in the soft moonlight. Their pockets stuffed full of trinkets, they would finally give in to the suffering summer heat and the bugs that crawled their way beneath children's collars. The boats would be loaded up, and the treasure would be returned to the Sprunt home to be sorted and spread out on the carpet.

Only after the coast was clear would the older teens come out of the reeds with their now empty sacks. Once full of the coins and cosmetic jewels, fake pearls and paste diamonds collected by Dr. Worth on his travels back home to Wilmington, the teens had arrived earlier to salt the sand with treasures for the little ones. Then they hid in the darkness, making scary sounds in the night to make the kids think the ghosts were just outside the ring of lights from the lanterns.

Every five years Dr. Worth would return, and every time he had a new map, always to the authentic treasure, and always guaranteed to find the prizes of Kidd's long hidden cache. The young children that once participated in the hunt would grow up to be the ones that would hide the rewards, taking their place in the chain of events.

James Sprunt would pass on in 1924, and Dr. Worth would leave this earth by 1936, with neither publicly acknowledging ever finding the treasure of Captain William Kidd. Most think that the treasure was never there, but buried closer to his home in New York. Others think it was long washed away or buried deep in the sands, spread out by the shifting islands until it was forever lost.

But there was a small bald hill on Money Island long ago, where a small copse of trees once stood. After the passing of Dr. Worth, found on the island, buried in the sands there, far from where the kids explored and treasure hunters dug, were five bottles of rum, not opened, but half consumed. They came from different countries, all with strange labels and languages, all different, all separated by five years of distillation.

Perhaps Dr. Worth knew just where the treasure was after all. He just didn't want to take it from the spirits of pirates long ago.

The Last Pirate Of North Carolina

Desperate times call for desperate measures. They also call for a bit of skill and luck, which seems to have run out on this group of pirates. Except for one.

In what may seem like a footnote to piracy, John Vidal is considered to be the last pirate ever to sail the waters of North Carolina. Of course, this statement is filled with hyperbole, as many later tales would show. But there is much more to the few simple acts of piracy by a man long forgotten and barely remembered.

Mostly because he's probably not the important one in the story. John Vidal is hardly even a footnote. His crew has been forgotten from tales and legends. He wasn't even successful in his acts, and he wasn't much of a pirate to begin with.

It is only because of one person, hardly a pirate at all, that John Vidal has any reason to grace the history of piracy.

In the spring 0f 1727, John Vidal was living a life of struggle along the coast of North Carolina. Life on the rugged shores were usually desperate, almost a day to day battle to merely stay alive for some. It is a story that barely

19

changed for hundreds of years. Vidal had made the acquaintance of Thomas Farley. Farley had found his way to the New World by force. He and his wife Martha had been convicts in England, sold to be slaves in the New World, but had escaped their debt to society, and moved on. Martha was living in the South Carolina colony, while Thomas looked for some way to move from destitute poverty. He found it with Vidal, along with two other men, Edward Coleman and Thomas Allen, who probably had been pirates in the past.

The four men staked their claim in the same stormy waters that Blackbeard himself once hunted, hid, and then died. From the shores of Ocracoke, Vidal sailed with his crew of ne'er do wells. Using what was ostensibly a boat but really nothing more than a sailing canoe, the men found their way out to a small craft that they pillaged for what they could. Later they would also take from a ship that had stranded and had been abandoned. Feeling their oats, Farley took their craft to get his wife and children.

Martha and the two offspring would join the crew, if by joining meant being placed on the same boat. The pirates would have some luck in May of 1727, even if it was short term, as they took what to them was probably a trophy in the schooner *Anne and Francis*. The trophy tarnished quite quickly, though. Vidal was in a rowboat with three prisoners from the ship when they quickly overpowered him and took him prisoner in a reversal of fortunes. They would turn him over to local authorities.

Seeing the writing on the wall, though the pirates probably couldn't read, Edward Coleman and Thomas Allen both attempted to return to the shore and blend in, finding shelter and somewhat more legal work on land. They would also be turned over when the locals informed on the men. The Golden Age of Piracy was long over. No one admired the criminals of crimes long ago, and certainly not if they were taking from local ships.

Curiously, Thomas Farley would disappear, never to be seen again.

He abandoned his wife Martha and children to the whims of the waves, as well as to the usually unforgiving courts when it came to the disposition of captured pirates.

North Carolina at the time had little in the way of Admiralty Courts, the maritime court system that dealt with pirates and seagoing law, and with the coastal events being close enough to the Virginia colony, the captured pirates were turned over to Williamsburg, where they could receive their trial. Coleman, Allen, and Vidal were all quickly convicted. There was by this era no patience for the nonsense of piracy, especially this petty and irritating pilfering of small ships and wrecks. Vidal's two accomplices were run out and run up a tree, hanged until dead. Vidal somehow escaped the noose, even though the colonial governor of Virginia at the time, Robert Carter, saw no redeeming qualities in the man. He wrote to the North Carolina governor, Richard Everard, "I must own to you I have very little Compassion for persons Convicted of his Crime ... It appeard very plainly to me from the Testimony against him (Vidal) as well as the rest that his heart was fully prepared for perpetrating the blackest of Vilianys, Altho the designe was laid with the greatest

Improbability of Success." Governor Carter obviously thought very little of Vidal, seeing him as quite a villain, but also seemingly incapable of succeeding in bringing about a New Golden Age of Piracy from the windswept Ocracoke shores.

However, in an act of benevolence thought to make him look better in the public eye, Carter, who had served only about one year as governor, granted Vidal a temporary stay of his death sentence. Newly appointed Lieutenant Governor for North Carolina William Gooch followed suit. He wrote to England asking for clemency for Vidal, which was granted in September of 1727, and Vidal was pardoned. He must have taken advantage of his renewed freedom, for he disappeared into the historical ether, never heard from again.

Martha Farley fared, well, better would be a relative description. She was judged to be part of the crew, and thus a pirate by definition. She testified that she only thought her husband had been taking Coleman and Allen back to their home in North Carolina, and was surprised by the first act of piracy while she was aboard the little craft. Still, Martha was used to listen in on the captive sailors' conversations, reporting their plans to Vidal.

With Martha Farley being the sole caretaker for two young children, as her husband had run off and never caught, the courts looked favorably upon her. Not wanting to orphan two kids, as well as having to be responsible for the children, the courts forgave her actions. They sent her back to South Carolina with a small stipend. The money, along with women's shoes stolen from a sloop's captain by her husband, were the bulk of the rewards the crew gained from their short lives of pirates on the North Carolina coast.

Curiously, Martha Farley, while a bit of a footnote in North Carolina pirate history, is an important lesson and reminder in the life of buccaneers. Often, sailors would be shanghaied into service, sometimes referred to as "handspike hash." A sailor would find the working end of a handspike, a wooden stake used to turn a windlass or tighten a line, placed upon the back of their head, rather forcefully, a hard strike meant to knock the doomed sailor unconscious long enough to get him on board and asleep until well underway. When he awoke with a handspike hash headache, he was put to work. Ship crews were often fulfilled with men this way. What they discovered was that married men would work very hard to get off the ship at the first opportunity to get back to their wives, and were not dependable sailors, whether they were kidnapped or hired.

Obviously Martha Farley and her family was an exception to the rule.

Or more likely Thomas Farley really was as worthless as he seemed.

So Thomas Farley escaped and George Vidal goes down as the last pirate of North Carolina, at least for a while.

Of all of them, Martha Farley may actually be the one with the most intriguing story. She was able to free herself from a useless husband, be freed from a court generally intolerant of pirates, with pay, even, and then get back to her home with her kids.

Vidal is named the last pirate of North Carolina, but he was just one of many. Martha Farley was the last female pirate from the state, and she kind of got away with it.

Captain Horatio Sinbad

Kids dream of being pirates when they are little. This is what happens when a dream becomes reality.

Pirates are bloodthirsty, vicious creatures, right? Full of only anger and hate, their blood as sour as vinegar, and the only thing lacking in their ship's cupboard is remorse. Pirates are well known for being barbarous and cruel in their short but dangerously vibrant lives. They usually don't live long, but they also don't live with regret.

Captain Horatio Sinbad was going to follow one of those pirates' fates, while bucking the other one.

Like many kids, young Horatio Sinbad was fascinated with the colorful life of pirates, when their lives seemed colorful, and not so much cutthroat. Living life on the sea, in command of your world as far as the eye can see, where the entirety of your existence stretched from the bow to the stern of the ship you commanded. It would go where ever the skipper's hand turned the ship's wheel, and you worked under no one else's flag but your own. It is a dream of every teenager, whether it's a car on the open road, or in this case, a ship at sea.

It didn't entirely matter that he was in Michigan, where it was much easier to get a fast American car than it would be to find a sailboat. And it wasn't the late 1600s, but the 1960s. He wasn't even Sinbad, let alone Captain Sinbad, at 19 years old, when he started building his pirate ship in his backyard in Detroit.

But what made a landlubbing swab of a teenager into a far flung buccaneer? There just isn't much in the way of schools to learn how to be a pirate.

Let's just say he got on the job training.

Before he was Captain Sinbad, he was Ross Morphew, just a kid from Detroit who, like most kids, enjoyed Disney movies. At 7 years old, he saw the film *Treasure Island*, and became fascinated with pirate life and lore. He would built his first boat at 11, and lose it soon after when it capsized as he sailed it in a lake.

At 16, he saw an ad in *Yachting* magazine looking for crew of a Caribbean schooner. Throwing a rope from his second story window, he ran away from his home, making his way to St. Lucia in the British Virgin Islands by hitchhiking, flying, whatever it took. When he finally arrived, he had almost no money, no place to stay, and only a return ticket as his last lifeline. When he showed up to meet the skipper, Captain Walter Boudreaux, a rough and tough no nonsense leader of sailing men, the captain was sure when he saw this skinny Detroit teen that young Ross would not survive two weeks.

But Boudreaux gave him a chance, and Ross showed that he knew his way around the long, low slung brig that was used for weeklong charter cruises for the rich visitors to the Caribbean islands. He was into sailing the boat. It was more than just a job to him; it was a lifestyle. And the captain quickly saw the talent in the young teen.

But it would take a bit of violence to truly earn his position.

A crew member had to stay on board when the ship was at anchor, and since Ross was new to the island, and had no family like the other local men that sailed with him, he stayed on ship. As he slept, someone came aboard. He heard a man stomping across the ship, going through the wine bottles to steal a few. Ross grabbed a belaying pin, snuck up on the miscreant in the dark, and whacked him good on the back of the head.

It turned out to be his captain.

After a bit of being chased around the ship by his angry and somewhat head hashed skipper, who was known around all of St. Lucia as the toughest, meanest and most hated man on the islands, cooler and more healed heads prevailed.

The next day Captain Boudreaux sat everyone down on the boat, and declared to all the older men that the sixteen year old boy was now first mate. Everything he said goes. And not to mess with the kid, because he was a killer. He had caved the head in of poor Captain Boudreaux, and the skipper had the lump to prove it.

That's how he began his career, but that's not how he got his name.

Living on a boat in a tropical island meant that Ross was growing a beard, turning blond, and getting fit and tanned.

So, one of his jobs, since he was both first mate and more trustworthy than the other crew members, was to take Captain Boudreaux's children in the launch to and from school. The kids, like most on the island, spoke a wonderful patois, a French creole, and the children had a hard time saying his name. But he looked a lot like someone they were reading about in a kids book, Sinbad the Sailor. So they started calling him Sinbad.

And Sinbad was born on a Caribbean shore.

Sinbad stayed a year and a half in the Caribbean, living a life many would dream about. He got a pittance for pay, but he had a bunk to sleep on, food, clothes, laundry, everything was provided, so thirteen cents an hour wasn't too bad. But all good things come to an end.

As a teenager, he had to go back to Michigan to finish high school. It would have been easy in the 1600s to run off to sea; by the 1960s, a young man had to get his diploma first.

And in Detroit, after high school, it meant working for General Motors, the same place his father, an engineer with the company, worked.

But even there, the lure of the sea called to him. At 19, he began building his own boat, and not a little sailboat this time. He began the construction of a full on ship, the *Meka*. The name was a Hopi word meaning meaning Stout, Loyal Companion. The name seemed fitting for a boat he was going to trust with his life. It didn't come together in a day. Building a ship in a garage had its drawbacks, and not only because salt water was nowhere to be found, with only the Detroit river nearby.

Horatio Sinbad at least had some things going for him. His father was not only an engineer, but also a talented woodworker, and young Sinbad grew up with the tools. He took engineering classes in high school and at the large technical college in Detroit. He found plans for wooden boats in magazines, and contacted other builders for help by writing letters and calling. This would be decades before the benefit of email and the internet. He even got offered a job teaching boatbuilding in Massachusetts. But the call to be a pirate was too strong. He finished the *Meka* and off he went, looking for adventure with his high school sweetheart wife. Second star to the right, and straight on till morning.

He began a life of modern classic piracy, living aboard the ship. He found his way from Detroit to Lake Erie, and then to the St. Lawrence Passage, a 2,300 mile waterway that allowed passage to the Atlantic Ocean. The Great Lakes were beautiful during summer, but summer wasn't long enough there. Sailing a ship on the lakes in the summer was pure joy, but being frozen on a lake in the winter was not. So the Atlantic called, with its warm waters.

Along the way he legally changed his name to suit his job, and Captain Horatio Sinbad had found his home on the sea.

Pirates don't plan much. They follow the wind to whichever way it flows, pretty much. If they want a secluded hidden beach, they find one. If they want to ransack a harbor town, they make sure the powder is dry.

They also don't plan on storms.

The *Meka* would get caught in a huge storm and be lost off of Bermuda. The Coast Guard would rescue Captain Sinbad and his wife, but the ship was too damaged to make any repairs.

It was back to Detroit, and back to building a bigger and better *Meka II*.

That low square sailed brig would be his home from then on. He sailed the coasts from Canada to the Caribbean in her, finding homes where ever he found jobs. With his skill in boat building, Captain Sinbad was in high demand. It even got him to his current home.

So Captain Sinbad didn't really plan on making Beaufort, NC his home. He had been working on a boat in Ft. Lauderdale, and when the owner took it north with only a few bits left to finish, he called Sinbad. He asked if the pirate sailor would like to come up and finish the work. He would like this little town in North Carolina called Beaufort. He could even find a nice place to dock the *Meka II*. After raising four kids onboard the *Meka II*, perhaps having a plank to walk ashore became a little more appealing back in 1973.

So Beaufort became his home port, and Captain Horatio Sinbad, scourge of the seas, a man who could not be held down to any place but the helm of his ship, had a slip in Spooner's Creek. And Beaufort was a perfect fit for a pirate. They had a pirate invasion every year, and just needed a real pirate. He was already dressed for the part, which helped.

Beaufort was happy to have him. Before Captain Sinbad and the *Meka II* showed up, all they had were shrimp boats and shotguns. Here was a real pirate, with a real pirate ship, and eight real pirate cannons. He came ready to party.

The party had actually started before Captain Sinbad had sailed into town. In 1960, the town started the celebration, but the original event happened in 1747. The original invasion really only had pirates if you looked at them from the land. From the sea, they probably saw themselves as vicious naval troops for Spain. This was long after the old Golden Age of Piracy, and the only pirates around were privateers, granted the privilege of fighting the English colonies from the Spanish port of St. Augustine. Under the papers of the Spanish king, Philip V, these pirates sailed into undefended Beaufort and took ships, then came back on August 26 and took over the whole town.

They held it for almost a whole... day. Colonial militiamen were rounded up and the town was taken back by the soldiers.

The celebratory Pirate Invasion that happens every year in Beaufort actually lasts longer, occurring over an entire weekend.

Captain Sinbad became a notable fixture in the town, whether it was for the pirate invasion, or running his cruises where he gave lessons in piracy. He offered more than the usual sunset cruises. Captain Sinbad did two week sailing trips for 12-16 year olds, where they lived onboard. They would make their own sea bags, learn the art of square rigged sails, wear a full uniform, and learn about fighting and sea battles at maritime events up and down the Atlantic coast. They even once took Miss North Carolina and her retinue captive from a coast guard ship. The planned attack went well until the captain and crew told her they were sailing off for Bermuda instead of returning her. She ultimately caught on to the joke and embraced the pirate life, if only for a few moments.

It's a good thing he had trained crews to help man the *Meka II*. To be a true pirate, or at least a privateer, any captain needs a letter of marque. And Captain Sinbad was no different. Starting in the 1970s, be petitioned President Gerald Ford, a fellow Michigander, for a privateer's license. He even got state senators and governors involved. Finally, in 1986, President Reagan signed a note giving Captain Sinbad legitimacy. In a carefully worded statement, as normally letters of marque come through Congress, the president allowed for Sinbad and his ship to attack the enemies of the U.S. "only if called upon."

The call of the sea, the fresh salt air and ocean breezes all have kept Captain Horatio Sinbad young and healthy through the years. He traveled to the Caribbean, becoming a literal Pirate of the Caribbean, in the flesh, and still hosts pirate invasions, including one on the more isolated Bald Head Island, where normally the only access is by ferry, but the port welcomes a pirate or two at the end of July. He participates in the Beaufort Invasion still, but is a self-described "hired gun."

And if Captain Sinbad raised a family onboard, he now had grandchildren. His kids have grown up, but they grew up where their backyard was wherever the boat put in, or wherever the horizon ends. And now he has grandchildren that have walked the decks of the *Meka II*. The young swabs made a whole new generation of pirates for the North

Carolina coast. And Captain Horatio Sinbad has not only a growing legion of friends, family, and factions, he has accomplished something most other pirates never have.

He got to grow old and keep his head.

The Last Ballad Of Simon Fernando

He was a rogue, a pilot, a troublemaker, a swine, a mapmaker, and a fighter. He was also a pirate and a father.

They called me a pirate."

Simon Fernandes ruminated on the remark. Portugal, his place of birth, saw him as an expatriate. Spain, who trained him, considered him a traitor. England, his home since 1573, saw him as a skilled pilot, but still a foreigner. Few of them cared much for him as a person. But as a sailor, there was none that could match his talent.

Still...

"They called me a pirate," he repeated, looking down at the young boy at his knee. The child was the face of his father, as well as an image of his grandfather, who now stood before him. *Ser a cara seu avô.*

"They were correct."

At this stage in his life, Simon Fernandes, born Simão Fernándes in 1538, "So long ago?" he pondered, figuring his current age in his head, had little left to prove. He stood on the green crinkled hills of his home island of Santa Maria in the Azores. It was where he had started his life, long ago, before moving to Spain to study seamanship and sailing.

Once in Spain, he had quickly moved from a *marinero* who served the *Casa de Contratación* for Spain and Philip II, to a well skilled pilot, navigator, and mapmaker. He sailed for Spain, using his talents well, making maps of the New World coasts. "While others followed the route of that Italian, Colombo, I was the one that charted up the coast of America," he explained to the boy. His maps showed intricate detail. Those maps he made would be his downfall and his rebirth.

"If you were a pilot for Spain," he explained to his grandson, "you and all sailing ships were expected to turn over twenty percent of their profits to the *Casa*. They guarded their power, and their maps, like the King cherished his gold and jewels. The *Casa* had their *Padrón Real*, the Royal Register, the official, yet supremely secret, map of all lands and seaways." Simon's eyes glinted in the sunlight. He could see the wonder in his grandson's eyes. That map was the reason that Spain had held the oceans in its greedy, calloused hands.

Simon Fernandes had seen the *Casa* and its officials do the taking, while he and the other *marineros* did the actual taking. He had charted the coasts, and the Spanish took his maps and put it to theirs, and then parceled it all out, at a fee of course.

"Is that when you left Spain?" his grandson asked.

Simon could tell that his grandson, like his son long before, had fallen into his tale of piracy and adventure. It was now Simon Fernandes' time to tell.

When Simon had met John Challice, "the *notorious* John Challice," Simon would say, the English pirate had been successful in the pilfering of Latin ships in the Atlantic. Simon Fernandes had taken his well drawn maps, the cherished tools of the *Casa de Contratación* and Spain, and left with the pirate Challice for the more welcoming world of England.

"We were able to take, and no one would take from us," he explained. Simon left out the tariffs that the queen and the shipowners all levied on him and Challice. They were small costs in comparison to the rewards he was able to get from the Spanish fleet coming back dripping with gold from the New World. "Using my maps," he added with emphasis.

Simon began walking down a beaten path from his home. His grandson followed. The two were devoted to each other, with the boy hanging on the words of each tale his grandfather told, and the old man delighted to relive his exploits with a willing and captivated audience.

"Is that when you went to the New World with the colonists?" the boy asked. He had heard the tale before, but there was always something new his grandfather would add. He had learned never to doubt the old man, for he had done tremendous things in his many years.

"Not at first," Simon explained. "Before I left for England, while others were sailing to la Florida, I was marking the unexplored coast. It was I who discovered the bays and islands where the English are attempting to settle now. I knew of this place they wanted to go, Roanoke, they named it, after the natives there.

"I had been there before, you know," he glanced at his grandson. The boy lit up. A new part of the story! "Years before, I had taken several ships there, in a plan to unload six hundred men on those horrendous islands to start a military colony. This would be my second trip, the first being a scouting expedition. I was the pilot, of course, but Grenville was captain. He insisted we scour the coast farther south. I had warned him not to get close to the shore. There it was not like the English channels and cliffs. The bottom was shallow, with hidden islands under the water that would reach up and grab  ships," he gestured with his hand, reaching for the boy. His grandson squealed as he easily escaped the grasp. "See? You will be a good pilot one day. You know to avoid the dangers, to find the deep waters, to see the paths in the seas.

"Grenville did not.

"He saw only his own path. He insisted we get closer, which led to one of the ships with most of the supplies getting stranded. We had to lighten the ship to save it, as it would have broken apart in the rough surf. I had warned them, Grenville and his lieutenant, Ralph Lane, of the dangers of this inlet, but they wanted to see for themselves. They made a foolish decision. But I learned from them," he said, with a mix of a smile and a grimace. It was a lesson, for good and ill.

"Were you punished?" the boy asked. He had seen how other boys were not careful, how they made mistakes, they were foolish, like his grandfather said, and they would regret that foolishness. He, too, learned a lesson.

"Punished?" Simon laughed. It would be hard to explain politics to the young boy, but he would have to know soon enough. "Certainly, Grenville and Lane wanted to blame me for the loss of the supplies. But they needed me to sail them back to England. And when we returned, they complained about the loss. But Sir Fancis Walsingham, who was the secretary of state for England, and Sir Walter Raleigh, who paid for the expedition, they did not complain. They knew the cost of some seeds and blankets were nothing compared to the cost of a ship!"

Then Simon let another sly smile slip. "Do you know who else did not complain?" He waited for a moment to spring this part of the tale.

"Who?!"

"Queen Elizabeth."

His grandson's eyes went wide. The old man had known the queen of England. "Yes, boy, the queen knew the value of a ship, and of a good pilot. It was at her word that I was put in charge of the colony expedition. She trusted no other." Simon huffed himself up to make him bigger, like the story he told. "She knew that I would get the ship safely, and quickly there, and back. She knew the value of the ship and the pilot," he repeated.

"What was it like when you got there?"

"Oh, it was nothing like this," Simon swept his hands across the vista of Santa Maria. Here, the lands were green, sharp, pointed with ancient volcanoes, mild breezes, and wide, round, protected bays. The Azores were a safe place, safe as a mother's arms. "Roanoke was a wild land. It was full of trees. You could barely walk with your arms out," he stretched his arms wide in illustration, "without touching one of the soft towering pines that grew there.

"It was hot, sunny, a thick place. The island sat in a wide shallow bay. We had to row in to land, but we could have as easily walked, the water was only to here," he touched his knee. "But it was as good as it would be. The land had trees for felling, and the land beneath was flat." The boy looked at the pointy crenellated peaks of the Azores; he couldn't imagine a flat piece of land. "And the beaches, soft sand, water filled with fish and shells. It seemed ideal.

"Except that it wasn't." Simon continued. "We had taken with us two of the natives, young men, named Manteo and Wanceese," the boy laughed at the names. Simon quietly reproached him, "But those *were* their names," he said quietly, "or at least how they said them."

He continued with his tale. "We had taken them to England and back. They had learned our language, and had pledged to support the colony. But when we arrived, we met with Manteo's people, who explained that the fresh water had begun to dry up, and that game had moved from the land. The colonists discussed moving on to the *Baya de Santa Maria*, a bay I had discovered, but I quickly put an end to that discussion.

"I had already dealt with these men, foolish, like I had said, and not dependable. I had a contract to deliver them to Roanoke, and no farther! I had warned them before we left that the land would be harsh, that they should not be taking women and children. English children," he corrected himself. Portuguese children would have fared much better, he thought. "This was no land for families, it was no home. But they had insisted in England we leave with the tide. Their leaders, Ananias Dare, John Borden, tried to make their arguments with other ways," he made fists with his old, calloused hands, "but they were not persuasive." Simon laughed at the memory of the two men, a bricklayer and a farmer, trying to fight him, and failing. "What was persuasive was the money Raleigh paid me." He looked back at his home, a large white walled building with a brown tiled roof. It was one of the largest on the island. "He paid well," Simon said.

"But when we arrived in the New World, they expected me to carry them on, past this land, to another. And then another. I had a job, to pilot them to Roanoke. I had a duty, to my crew first, to my ship as much, to return to England. The colonists were supplies. I had delivered the supplies, and no one would say I had not."

"What happened to them?" his grandson wondered.

Simon Fernandes was silent for a moment. He wasn't sure what to say. His little descendant, still young and innocent, would learn soon enough the vagaries and difficulties of the world. He knew he was fortunate. Most sailors did not live long lives. The years were dirty, painful, thankless, and short. He had seen men grow old quickly, from a sixteen year old boy climbing the lines to a twenty years old, salted, shriveled, brown, more leather than his own boots.

Others would age differently. The men who cast the metal, they were paid well, but soon they, too, would begin to cough and choke from the black smoke that gave them their English names. He had known many a Smith. And they, too, would die.

Who knows what happened to those colonists? He barely thought about it. He had learned his lesson, well and early. He delivered them, came back, and continued his life.

"I do not know." It was all he said. "It was a life full of risks. They knew it. I told them.

"I warned them." Simon became quiet and wistful.

"You never went back?"

"No. There would be nothing to go back to."

Simon walked his grandson down toward the docks in Vila de Porto. The ships sat waiting, waiting for crew, tides, or wind. There they would find Simon the Younger, Simon Fernandes the son, the offspring of the greatest pilot of all time. And the young boy's father.

Simon Fernandes thought about the choices in his life. He had been a sailor, a *marinero*, a pilot, and, yes, a pirate. He had been hated, called swine by the English, solely because he was a foreigner, a Spaniard, "they always got that wrong," thought the Portuguese.

Once he came back to England, the nation, his nation, the one he had adopted, converted into, married into, had children, was at war with Spain and the king. With no more ships sailing to the New World, he had taken the employment he had loved, fighting and hunting the Spaniards that had taken from him more than he gave. He fought against their Armada, and won. He took a ship and sailed to take their plunder from the New World. He was called a privateer by the English, by the queen, and a pirate by Spain and his homeland of Portugal.

He knew he was aging, sailing was getting more difficult. He had already outlived the young men who climbed the lines or made the cannons. He saw the benefits of his long life as he handed his grandson off to his son, a grown man, a reputable pilot and captain himself.

It was the same port he had come in, now thirteen years earlier, for the last time. He had decided to end his career, whether it be pilot or pirate. He had a son and wife, he had more money than he needed. He only needed a home, so he had found one. He had sailed in, told everyone that Simon Fernandes had sailed off to attack Spanish ships in the New World, and had disappeared.

The world was fooled. It was easy with the foolish. No one lived that long. Simon Fernandes, Simão Fernándes, Simon Fernando, all those names he was known by, Swine, pilot, pirate, privateer, all those people, they were all but dead to the world. It had been a good life.

As he watched his son and grandson prepare for their own journey to Spain, to make their own lives, he wondered, for a moment, how he would be remembered. But that was for the future to decide.

It had been a good life, so far.

For Simon Fernandes, it would be a good life, still.

A Healthy Spot And A Lucky Shot

William Howard was a lucky man. He had lived long enough to accumulate some wealth and own an island. He also served with one of the most infamous pirates in history. Both of their names would be preserved, for very different reasons.

Fortune is a fickle mistress. It was something that William Howard knew all too well.

He looked out over his expansive land, once almost the entirety of Ocracoke Island. In the distance, his sheep jumped and twitched at the biting flies that had been brought by the west winds. The strong warm breeze that brought the flies out of the marshes and sounds to bite at his livestock also blew the flies and mosquitoes away from him as he sat on the shade of his porch. What was good fortune for the man was poor for the sheep.

Fortune had been good to him, generally. He had his rough patches, but here he was, living comfortably on an island, at a very ripe old age. How old was he? One hundred? Older? His memory may not be quite what it used to be, but he still remembered most of his life, the good fortune and the bad.

He had bought Ocracoke Island decades ago, back in, about... 1750? He had been old then. By that time people mostly knew him as a wealthy landowner in Bath, the inland port town where his family had been from. When he bought Ocracoke, most of the people who had known who he was were already dead. The few who thought they knew who he was, well, they thought *he* was already dead. There was no way that he could be the same William Howard, *the* William Howard who had sailed with the notorious Blackbeard, Edward Teach, the dreaded pirate who met a bloody end in the waters just to the south of the island.

He may be getting older, not remembering everything as well. But he certainly remembered that he was a pirate.

Of that he was sure.

Ocracoke was a healthy spot to grow old, as long as you could survive adulthood. William Howard had done that, though he wasn't sure just how well he had done. He had certainly run his share of risks.

Good fortune had blown his way.

But he knew that you sometimes couldn't tell if that wind was for good or ill until after the storm was done.

William Howard had been young, but old enough, when he had taken in with Teach and his crew. His home in Bath had been a favorite port for scoundrels, pirates, sailors of all kinds. His father, Phillip Howard, had owned hundreds of acres of land all along the Pamlico River. Bath was a popular place for pirates to hide. Not only was it a safe inland port, but North Carolina was well known for its political shelter of pirates as well. Which made the town a good port for Captain Benjamin Hornigold. Hornigold sailed into Bath, was welcomed because of his gold, and he had then welcomed the young Howard aboard his ship as quartermaster. Later, in 1718, Hornigold again returned to Bath. This time along with his partner, Teach, now well known by his new moniker, Blackbeard.

William Howard, already a skilled sailor, had the skills of a businessman even at his young age. Blackbeard saw within him a host of positive talents. He was first of all trustworthy, and smart, a talent on board a ship, an even hand at a ship's wheel, and most notably, had a thirst for piracy and the rewards it would bring.

He had signed on early in 1718, which was a good time for him, and his captain. At that time, Blackbeard had five ships, and needed a skilled quartermaster. He had taken *La Concorde*, a French slave ship, and turned the big craft into his flagship, renaming it the *Queen Anne's Revenge*. The *Revenge* had been Howard's ship.

Howard was brought back from his reverie by a sharp sting at his neck. A mosquito had landed and searched out some of his blood, a sweet sip for the vampiric little creature. The wind had shifted.

It reminded him of another spilling of blood, on his ship, long ago. Another bit of fortune, good or bad, he wasn't sure.

William Howard wasn't the only pirate of note to serve under Teach. He remembered another of the quartermasters who served, trusted lieutenants that were a cut above the common sailors that came and went with whatever port their ship called home at the moment. Israel Hands was an officer, if they had officers, on one of the ships in Blackbeard's fleet. He served aboard the *Adventure*, a smaller sloop, but a good one. He was handy, willing to climb the lines, steady on his feet even in a storm, and could drink other men under the table with ease. Hands was not one to be trifled with. Even Howard kept an arm's length from the hardened sailor.

He was, however, not hardened enough to stop a bullet.

One time, at one of the many ports they called upon, Teach, for no reason it seemed, pulled one of the many pistols he carried loaded about him, and shot Hands in the knee. It would take time for the shock and pain to set in. Hands, stunned at the nonchalant way in which the shooting had happened, asked the commodore Blackbeard why he had shot him.

Teach had explained he was trying to shoot a swab, one of the many sailors on the ships, but missed. He went on, explaining, "If I don't kill one of them every now and then, they will forget who I am."

The wound would heal, as best as wounds did without a doctor's care, but Israel Hands would from that time forward suffer from the shot. He could only walk with a cane or crutch, and his pirating days were certainly over.

Bad fortune had blown Hands' way, it had seemed, when the musket ball had missed its target and hit Hands in the knee.

But then, William Howard knew what had happened next, so "maybe not," he thought.

Then, rubbing at the bite on his neck, "maybe so."

Time was also a fickle mistress.

William Howard served with Blackbeard until May of 1718. At that time, the colonial governor of North Carolina had offered a rather handsome pardon to any pirate who would come to claim it. With the alternative being a neck stretched at the end of a rope, a slow and undignified death, William Howard had wanted to take the pardon. He could easily return to Bath a rich man, even without his father's help, and live a comfortable life of ease. Other pirates thought the same. Even Teach, now a successful pirate for about a year and a half, was intrigued.

But all pirates were greedy.

The *Revenge* was run aground, the treasure moved, and several of the crew, including William, had gone ahead to take the proffered amnesty from Governor Eden. William Howard pledged never to take to piracy again. "And I kept that promise," he said to himself, knowing it wasn't entirely true.

Teach had taken the same pledge, but he left Bath mere months later, and met his end right here in Ocracoke.

William Howard had lived on.

He had his own share of close calls of wild Miss Fortune playing with him. He had been arrested soon after in Virginia, thinking he was free from prosecution with his North Carolina pardon, and happily confessed to all sorts of acts of piracy. "What were they going to do, hang me?" he laughed a dry, humorless laugh. They most certainly were. The North Carolina pardon held no sway in the more civilized Virginia, where they hanged people who thought they were free, and left the bodies to rot.

His execution was scheduled, but most of the royal marines and sailing captains were all busy with other issues. Most notably, someone had captured and possibly killed the most wanted pirate of the day. Blackbeard was dead, his head hanging from the bowsprit of a ship heading back to Norfolk.

The timing of the killing of Blackbeard, delaying his execution by a day, allowed for good winds again, as a ship sailed in carrying a formal message from King George himself. All pirates who wish it were granted great mercy from the king of England.

William Howard was a free man.

The wind had shifted again. "Both now and then," he remembered, as a breeze blew over the porch.

William hadn't gone straight back to Bath to become some gentrified land owner. Those inner coast lands may have money in them, but they also had more mosquitoes, more flies, and, "more heat," he remembered as the breeze turned from the west, and a more comfortable ocean breeze, full of salt, hit him square in the face. It was a familiar and pleasant feeling for the old sailor.

When he was freed, William had gone to the Bahamas. It was tough to get the pirate out of him, but he certainly wasn't going back to the Carolinas now. He had his freedom, but now there was an organized hunt for whatever pirates were left. The Golden Age of Piracy had ended when Teach had lost his head off Ocracoke's soundside beach.

But when he made it to the Bahamas, he had discovered he had a choice. A doctor was being tried for piracy, and William knew him, because he had been there when the doctor and Howard had served on the same ship. With the promise of immunity, William Howard had readily admitted he had taken poor Doctor John Howell against his will and made him serve aboard Benjamin Hornigold's ship. Howell was freed, as was William Howard.

Freed from the need to be a pirate. His conscience was no longer prepared for the dirty work, he had realized. He served as a sailor and quartermaster, but piracy was behind him by then.

And in the coming years, he profited from his long life. He had bought the entirety of Ocracoke Island, then almost immediately sold half of it off. It was the half to the south, where the water had run blood red at the beach, where Blackbeard and his crew had been killed or captured. William Howard wondered if the sailors had bothered to bury the bodies, or just threw them overboard, food for the crabs in the shallow sound.

He gave a shiver even in the warm air. Again, a strange bit of fortune.

He thought of Israel Hands, his one time contemporary. Both of them had escaped the clutches of piracy, and the prosecution of it. Hands was nearly crippled, no longer able to operate on a ship. When Blackbeard sailed to Ocracoke, he had to stay behind. He would be no good, a one legged man on an open sloop. Of all the crew, he was one of the few that escaped either the sword or musket ball, or worse, the hangman's noose.

But then Hands had disappeared. He had made his way to England and died soon afterwards, penniless and lost.

William Howard had taken his riches and moved to the coast. He knew Ocracoke to be a good and healthy place. He was living proof. Here he was, owner of half an island, herds of sheep and cattle and hogs, still standing at, what, a hundred years old? Older? Numbers didn't matter much now, he thought.

The sun began to set behind him. The wind shifted and swirled around him, coming from different directions at the same time.

Who knew what fortune would bring him in the future?

The Carroll A. Deering

It is a mystery what happened to the Carroll A. Deering. The vessel found her way to the Diamond Shoals off of Cape Hatteras with her crew missing, never to be found. No one ever discerned what had happened to the ship and crew. In the 1920s, could it really have been pirates?

Pirates only existed in the long ago past. Right? They had their time, back in the 1500s, right up until Blackbeard lost his head and everyone in the career decided to give up and take regular sailors jobs. After that, it just wasn't worth the risk to be a professional pirate anymore.

Certainly by the twentieth century, by the 1920s, after years of war, with the hope of peace now closer than ever, there would be no more pirates sailing the seas. Especially on the growing Atlantic coast off of North Carolina.

Surely no captain would ever expect to find a pirate ship on the horizon.

Definitely they would never expect to find them even within their own crew.

Would they?

Captain William Merritt was the skipper of the *Carroll A. Deering*, a beautiful five masted schooner. Painted a cool bright white, she sailed like a cloud on the calm water, and made good way in winds. Not exactly yar, she was made for hauling large amounts of goods safely from far away ports, not for high speed. But she was smooth, safe, and still new. The *Carroll A. Deering* was the flagship of the G.G. Deering line, named after the son of the owner. But the Deering, like all ships, was a *she*.

Captain Merritt was happy to be sailing her. He was bringing the ship in from Puerto Rico to Newport News, Virginia, in order to put together a crew for a trip down to Rio de Janeiro to deliver a load of coal and then return with the hold full of rare wood. There may be opportunity for stops in other places, too, with the promise of more exotic choice of goods from other island nations.

The addition of Merritt's son, well seasoned himself and definitely trusted, would make the trip easy, perhaps even pleasant. It certainly would be better than his last sail.

Captain Merritt had been the skipper of the *Dorothy B. Barrett*, which had been torpedoed near the end of World War I by a German U-boat. While the ship burned and sunk, Captain Merritt had gotten his crew into lifeboats, saving every soul on board.

So, with a crew of mostly Scandinavians, and his son to run them, Merritt set out from Virginia to warmer climates.

Unfortunately he fell ill and decided to return to port to get a new captain. It would also mean hiring a new first mate, since Merritt's son would be going ashore with his father.

So, Captain Willis Wormell, a retired sailing captain, was contracted for the trip to Brazil and back. The company separately hired Charles McLellan as first mate. The two did not know each other before the sail, but would learn intimately of each other's last nerve on the sail down to Rio.

They sailed for Brazil on September 8, 1920. Fighting the fall winds that would blow from the south, they arrived, notably without much complaint or incident, in Rio de Janeiro, at the end of November. After unloading the coal and waiting for any new cargo he could get, Captain Wormell gave the crew shore leave until the *Deering* was loaded. The crew took advantage of the freedom of a port city, and Wormell, at 66 years old, found more sedate company in the conversation of other captains he knew. He stated that he didn't entirely trust the crew, since he was unfamiliar with them. Scandinavians were particularly suspicious, as sailors fear their ability to whistle up an ill wind. But with his ship full, Wormell called all hands back to the Deering, and set sail for islands north.

Things must have gone worse for the ship, for as they reached Barbados, both captain and first mate were in foul moods. Barbados should have been a rollicking and wild port of call, with its main export of rum and sugar. But McLellan got excessively drunk that night, exclaiming how he hated the captain. "He won't let me discipline the crew without him butting in. He doesn't trust me to do my job." He would state in angry drunken revelry, "I'm going to get that captain before we get to Virginia."

For his part, Captain Wormell had no better feelings about McLellan. The first mate was right, Wormell didn't trust McLellan at all, and had been butting his head into the day to day work of the crew. So it was surprising that, after McLellan got thrown into a Barbadan jail, Wormell took pity and bailed him out.

The ship would sail into even more ominous winds as it headed north. January 9, 1921 would still be a new year for many, but it would be end for the *Deering* and crew. They just didn't know it yet.

It would be almost twenty days later that the ship would be seen again. This time it would be by the Cape Lookout lightship, anchored off the empty coast to warn ships off of the dangerous Lookout Shoals. The lightship keeper, Thomas Jacobsen, later told of several strange events that happened at the time. On January 28, 1921, the *Deering* passed near the lightship, where the keeper spied several men on the quarterdeck, an area usually reserved for the captain. A thin, younger man with bright red hair hailed the lightship through a megaphone, telling Keeper Jacobsen that the ship had lost its anchors in a storm. The strange figure spoke English in a distinct accent. He was certainly not the American Captain Wormell.

There was little Keeper Jacobsen could do other than make note of the passing and wish the ship luck in making way through the upcoming Diamond Shoals and the dreaded Graveyard of the Atlantic. His radio was out at the time. He would hopefully be able to hail another passing ship in the future to have them contact the Coast Guard to warn them of the *Deering* in distress. He did not have too wait long, but the events to come were even more curious.

Soon after the *Deering* passed, Jacobsen saw a large oil burning ship, a low, long modern ship with a smokestack, burning its marine gas and making dark clouds. Jacobsen tried to observe it with his binoculars but could see no name on it. He attempted to signal the ship, but it seemed to ignore his requests. He then sounded his steam whistle, a long call that could be heard clearly for miles. It was a call that couldn't be ignored. If the ship's whistle was sounded, by law any other ship had to respond to the call.

This strange ship simply turned away, off to sea, and disappeared into the salty mist, only leaving the sickening cloud of burnt fuel. It was an odd and disappointing series of events. Ominous, it was something that would come to haunt the story of the *Deering* in the future.

Another ship would later spot the *Deering* heading straight toward the Diamond Shoals of Hatteras, with no one on deck. They assumed the ship would see the Cape Hatteras light and turn to avoid getting stranded on the offshore sandbars. No one would purposefully steer themselves into those treacherous waters.

It would be three days later, January 31, 1921, when the *Deering* would be spotted for the last time. Coast Guardsman C. P. Brady would see the *Deering*, stuck on one of the outer shoals off of Cape Hatteras, being pounded by the relentless waves from storms offshore. Due to the high winds and waves, there was no way to get a rescue boat out to the *Deering* to save the crew. It would be days later when the lifesaving ships were able to make headway. When they finally arrived on February 4, they would discover that they shouldn't have worried. The *Deering* was completely, or almost completely, abandoned.

It was a strange sight to see. The ship had been damaged by the rough surf, but was probably in relatively shipshape condition when it was stranded. The sails were reefed, tied to the spars to reduce the surface in the high winds that it had faced the days before. The coast guard even found that food had been put out in the galley in preparation for the crew's next meal. The ship had all the signs of being fit for sail.

Until they went to the bridge.

There the coast guard found an even stranger sight. The ship's wheel had been broken to bits and the rudder controls were disengaged. The binnacle, a small post in the middle of the bridge that housed the ship's compass and other navigational tools, was crushed. The ship's log was removed, along with maps and sextant, all devices used to help divine the path the ship needs to take to find its way home to port.

In the crew quarters, all the clothes were gone as well.

The lifeboats were missing.

The ship had clearly been abandoned. The only living soul on board was the ship's cat, a healthy mouser who had the unique feature of being polydactyl; it had six toes on its paws.

The coast guard, disappointed after all the work they did to get aboard, made a point to rescue the cat. The feline would be the only part of the *Deering* mystery that left a positive mark on the island. The passionately voracious tom would go on to sire large numbers of feral hunters to the island.

The rest of the crew disappeared forever.

The *Deering* was too severely damaged to refloat and salvage. It was deemed a hazard to navigation, and was blown to bits, almost, about a month later so that it would not float out to sea.

The pride of the Deering company did not survive even two years at sea. Its hull would survive long enough to wash ashore in Ocracoke. The wood from the ship would be used to shore up the foundation of houses across the Hatteras coast.

The end of the *Deering*, though, was just the beginning of the mystery.

How could, in the 1920s, a ship so big and new, just have its crew disappear? The mystery deepened, and more and more government agencies began to investigate. The Navy was involved, along with the Commerce Department, the State Department, the U.S. Treasury, and the Justice Department. All had questions, worries, concerns. Soon, ideas began to form. But answers were harder to come by.

There were the obvious. The ship was simply abandoned in a storm, and the crew was lost to the horrors of a hurricane. As likely, possibly more so, was that the crew, led by McLellan who had pledged vengeance on the captain, had simply mutinied, killing the remaining faithful crew before abandoning the ship.

But there were other suggestions, many that held some water, salty it may be. Rather than just a hot blooded mutiny planned at the moment, there was evidence that the attack was planned. Bolsheviks, new communist activists loyal to the USSR, had suggested that agents train to infiltrate crews to take over ships and take them back to the fledgling nation.

But all the stories, the ideas, these suggestions, they all had just enough holes in them to let water in to leak. And a leaky ship, sooner or later, it sinks.

The *Deering* was in fine shape when boarded. The sails were intact, the hull had to take days of constant beating by Hatteras waves and finally an explosion with dynamite. There literally was food on the table. There seemed to be no reason to abandon ship into the risky and small lifeboats, especially when rescue from the coast guard was nearby.

Mutiny still seemed likely. McLellan hated his replacement captain, and Wormell was outspoken in his contempt of the First Mate. It would seem like an easy reach to assume the crew mutinied, killing Wormell. But they would have had to kill more than him. The rest of the officers would be loyal. Those would have to die, too. It would not be an easy task. And then, why did they abandon the ship? Especially in high seas.

One of the investigations done was an exhaustive search for the surviving crew. If they survived, the lifeboats would have washed up somewhere. The crew would appear in a port, even if it was as far away as Bermuda or back in the

Caribbean. No one, not a single soul, ever appeared again, living or dead. If it was mutiny, it served no purpose after a few hours passed.

Only the cat survived.

If the *Deering* had been the only mysterious disappearance on the North Carolina coast at the time, it would have just been marked up to just another victim of the Graveyard of the Atlantic. But other ships had also disappeared at the same time. The *Monte San Michele*, the *Esperanza de Larrinaga*, the *Ottawa*, and the oil burning ship *Hewitt*. While the pile up of missing ships all within a few days drew attention to the unexplained occurrences, the *Hewitt* was the most concerning, especially for the *Deering*.

Most of the ship losses were marked up to storms. Winter winds whipped up an oceanic death knell for ships in the Atlantic, especially the slow moving sailing ships like the *Deering*. But the *Hewitt* was a big steel hulled freighter, a steamer, meant to haul bulk sulfur in her hold. Not only was she well suited for rough Atlantic wasters, she, like the *Deering*, was heading away from the storms that took the other ships, not into them.

What was more interesting was that she fit the description of the mysterious ship that turned away the hail at the Cape Lookout Lightship.

It is speculated that the *Hewitt* was taken by pirates as a hefty prize for running illicit goods across the wide open Caribbean. When Keeper Jacobsen spotted the mysterious ship, his description closely matched the *Hewitt*.

S. S. Hewitt, Union Sulphur Co., Sabine, Texas

Did pirates come across the *Deering,* seeing it as an additional prize? That ship with its big open hull could carry a lot of rum during Prohibition's heyday. A single trip to an unmarked port would easily bring over a million dollars to the Caribbean rum runners. It is thought that the pirates that took over the *Hewitt* plotted with the crew of the *Deering* to take her, too. A fleet of rum runners would be better than a single ship. But the pirates discovered several things when they took the *Deering.* An unwilling captain was one thing, but adding more officers to the group that had to be gotten rid of would cause more problems. As would handling a sailing ship that needed more than the six or seven deck crew that were part of the mutiny and takeover.

After McLellan led his overthrow of the ship, they realized that the *Deering* was more of a reward than they could handle. They met up with the *Hewitt,* transferred over, and then did their best to cover up the dastardly deeds they did. Smashing the binnacle and breaking the controls meant the *Deering* would find her way into the teeth of the Diamond Shoals. She surely would break apart on the far off

63

bars, spilling water in and spilling out what little evidence of their piracy there was.

The pirates just didn't count on being spotted by the lightship off Cape Lookout. Which is why the *Hewitt* hid her name and never answered the hail. The mutinous crew on the *Deering* did what they could to make the ship seem like it was in distress, even loosing the lifeboats to sink in the offshore storm. They took all evidence, the log books and navigational maps that showed their track. The anchor lines were cut, and the emergency beacons had been lit and burned out, as if the ship was adrift. But there was no reason for the ship to not be under sail, if the captain and crew had so desired.

Perhaps it was pirates who took the *Deering*, taking the crew captive if they chose not to serve willingly, and forcing poor Captain Wormell and his faithful crew to walk the plank like in days of old.

It would be a mystery that would never be solved. The *Hewitt* disappeared forever, possibly steamed off to change her name, only to rust away on a Caribbean island or a swampy bayou in the Gulf of Mexico. The *Deering* had no happier a fate. After her stranding, a few fortunate locals were able to seize what little was of value, sails, some furniture, before the ship was blown to bits. Only the windlass from the ship still exists. It was pulled from wreckage and used as a gas station display until it found a home in a museum.

All that is left is the mystery. And the cats.

Blackbeard

Have you ever wondered about the thoughts that the great pirate Blackbeard had in his head? Look inside the mind of Captain Teach to see what he believed and what he knew to be legend as he contemplates his life to come.

I s North Carolina going to be my home?
It was a simple question that Edward Teach asked himself as he stood overlooking the Pamticough River from his house in the colony's capital of Bath. The town was flourishing, growing daily with more trade coming through the water. Or at least it had been, until the last few months. He wondered if he had anything to do with either change in events.

He looked at the chairs strewn around his shaded porch. They were a strange mix of eclectic fancy, but all different styles from different places, and all worn from too much abuse. He stood, not wanting to sit even if he was sore from the night before. A bit of wild debauchery and excessive rum had never hurt him before. He had no desire to sit down now.

His giant frame thanked him. It was always a little farther to fall, and a little more work to get back up. Teach was large in comparison to most men of the town. He stood a head taller than most others, with broad shoulders, long arms, and a solid torso. Even at his age, 38 years old if he remembered correctly, not that it mattered, he was still stronger than any man in the town, even ones half his age.

"Is this where I will sit?" he asked. He stroked his beard. It was getting long again. He had arrived in Bath in June of 1718, with the full intent of ending his former career and enjoying the lavish lifestyle he was able to bring from his glorious pay days. He had even cut and neatened his beard in order to minimize the striking appearance that went with his name, Blackbeard.

Now it grew.

He had to grow it back. He had gotten tired of the neat look he was forced to keep, the trimmed beard, the simple clothes of a well to do landowner. Teach had to get his name back. He couldn't let people forget who he was.

He wondered if he had forgotten who he was, just a few months ago, back in August. Now, by November, everyone knew of him again. That was the way he liked it.

He was still standing.

Teach thought about how he had gotten to where he was now, both a respected member of good society, and the most dreaded pirate of the Atlantic coast. Here in Bath, men talked in jovial, but banal, tones, "What was like like being a pirate?" with a smile and a laugh. They said it like being a farmer or a businessman was somehow better. Out on the ocean, sailing captains feared him, and governors wanted him dead, hanged by a gibbet on a pole somewhere. Neither appealed to him, but this life on land...

Teach shuddered.

His wife, his "wife," Mary, a sixteen year old girl who had fallen for his wealth and dark good looks had been almost sold off to him by her parents who were glad to be rid of her, and also hoped to bring back riches to their family, was somewhere in the house, remaining quiet. Teach had married her, smitten by her looks and willingness, as he had so many times before, only to grow tired of her as quickly as he had grown tired of life on land. She had become one of the main reasons to leave.

He had requested the opportunity to go to St. Thomas to acquire a commission to privateer for the English crown against Spain in the War of the Quadruple Alliance. England could make up wars and their names all they chose, Teach didn't care. If it gave him a chance to become a pirate again, they could call it whatever they liked.

He looked out over the water, leading away from his home, toward the east, and the open water of the Pamticough Sound, and farther out, to Occacoke and Portsmouth Island. The barrier islands with their windswept shores and scrub trees and open inlets to the ocean beyond, they almost seemed to call to him, teasing with cool salt sprays that kept the air mild and the prodigious mosquitoes at bay. How did he make the choice to be here, in Bath, instead of out there, on the islands, on the ocean, on his ship at sea?

"Is this going to be my home?" he kept saying it to himself, "How did I get here?"

As a boy, he had seen the big ships come and go from his home in Bristol, England. Back then, he hadn't been Blackbeard, since he couldn't raise a beard to save his life, and he wasn't even Edward Teach. He chose than name when he signed on to work a ship to the New World. He wasn't going to reveal who he really was, and no one cared that he gave a created name. That time, the world in which he had existed as a teenager, that world was a blur to him. Merchant ships, slavers, and armed sloops, they all were just a deck to him. He had particularly enjoyed the fighting part. He had found success in being a privateer during the War of Spanish Succession. The pay was better, the more democratic nature was certainly better than the slavish demands that British officers made upon the crews of their fighting ships, and he had nowhere else to go but up. The Caribbean was his oyster, and he was going to seize every pearl he could take.

It was there that he discovered the island of New Providence. He and few thousand other privateers turned pirates after a treaty was signed, ending all organized hostilities toward Spain. Now begins the *disorganized* hostilities, a young Teach would say. New Providence was the Republic of Pirates, an island free from any and all rules. No one lived there, not permanently, at least. The occasional trader and outfitter set up shops there to do repairs and sales, to provide a place to trade or buy food. The island had fresh water, a surprisingly necessary commodity. The island was a temporary vacation land, though the vast majority of the population lived on the water in their ships, a literal floating civilization, all just offshore.

New Providence was a wonderful location, just off the Florida Straits, and nearby enough to the shipping lanes for all sorts of merchant ships, laden with both treasure and necessities. They all would be ripe for the picking.

It was there that Teach would meet up with his first pirate captain, Benjamin Hornigold. Hornigold's fierceness was legendary, a true master at the art. He was laden with riches beyond comprehension. He quickly saw that Teach had skills beyond the normal swabs that worked the decks, and gave him command of his own sloop, a prize they had recently taken on one of their voyages of plunder.

Teach remembered the sloop well. He also remembered the crew. He had met William Howard at the time, and made him quartermaster. Howard was a skilled navigator, and ran a ship well. But when they had taken a ship from Madeira, the crew had gotten so feverish for the wine they had seized, Howard was all but forced to crack open the contents to give them a taste. The crew had insisted in taking another ship, the *Betty*, heading toward the Virginia colony, solely because it carried Madeira wine. They had sent it on its way without taking any other cargo.

Teach remembered well how the crew responded. Instead of berating them, he had drunk with them instead. He knew to reward the crew, to keep them happy, but also to understand who was captain.

Other pirates were not as fortunate.

"That was when I first met Bonnet," he thought. "Stede Bonnet, the *Gentleman Pirate!*" Teach laughed out loud at the term. Bonnet was neither of those. He was not even much of a captain or a sailor, really. He was a rich boy who saw the glamour in running away to the sea to be a pirate without learning the lines of the ship he bought first. He was called the Gentleman Pirate because of his fancy dress. His crew had thought much less of him, Teach remembered.

Hornigold and Teach had met Bonnet during this highly successful time in their life of piracy. They first met Bonnet on his ship he had so tactfully named the *Revenge*, as most sloops taken by pirates would be named. "I ended up doing almost the same thing," Teach admitted to no one on his porch. Bonnet's crew had grown dissatisfied with their "captain" and his lack of skills. His abusive nature, beating the crew for any imagined slight, also created a rift with the wealthy former landowner. But what most rubbed their sunburned skin wrong was that Bonnet had been a poor pirate. Their take was meager for all the work they had done. When the ships met at New Providence, the crew fairly begged Teach to take over the ship.

So Teach moved to the *Revenge*, Bonnet took over Teach's former ship, and Hornigold ran his sloop, the *Ranger*. They no longer had ships. They had a flotilla.

Three armed ships working together, or separate, would take what they wanted, and leave nothing left. That is what Teach thought, along with much of the crews of the three ships.

It was at this time that Teach, having given up the necessity of shaving and having a decent naval appearance on board a British merchant ship, had let his beard and hair grow. It came in raven feather black. With his tanned skin, dark eyes, tall, muscular frame, and wide shoulders, he was a forbidding sight. Women found his appearance to be nothing less than a smoldering fuse, something to light them on fire for a night, if only they could draw his attention. Like all sailors, he was starved for womanly attention, but when the women of the islands came to him, to sit on his lap or to put a hand in his purse, it did not matter, why would he say no?

"It had been a good time," he remarked, looking in his house. Still no sign of his wife now. She may not come out at all today.

"My crew would taunt me. They would say I would get married in every port.

"They were right," he chuckled inwardly, again. It was an open rumor in the islands that Teach had been married eleven times, "Fourteen now," he thought, figuring the math and the names of women. He had been married, depending upon how one defined marriage. Most of these "marriages" were merely convenient terms for him having a woman and a home to come to when he landed in an island. He had really only been married, he counted again, "three times?" he wondered. Certainly this last time, once in Beaufort, and at least once in Jamaica. Most of the rest were merely words spoken. He was captain, and as such, if he declared himself married, well, he was married, until he declared himself not married. It was very convenient when he met a newer, younger, more attractive bride to be.

Yes, he got along well on his looks, as well as by his sail.

"That was when Hornigold first called me Blackbeard."

The terrible moniker with which he was graced was from his former captain, who unimaginatively gave him the nickname. It stuck, easily, of course. It did not seem like much of a terrifying name to Teach. Not at first.

Hornigold had been fierce, yes, but he had morals, a bit of a code of conduct, still within him from his privateering days. Teach, Bonnet, Howard, and all the crews watched as fleets of English flagged vessels had sailed by, untouched by the pirate captain. He was still loyal to his country that had given him his privateer commission. Hornigold would not take an English ship.

The crew grew frustrated, Teach remembered. A pirate ship was a truly egalitarian community. The captain ran the ship, made decisions, helped distribute the loot, while others did their own trades. Pilots, navigators, quartermasters, they all had their own jobs to do, as did the lowliest swab who climbed the lines as a lookout. All had a voice in who ran the ship. When they grew tired of watching English ships passing, low in the water, slow, unarmed, ripe, but untouchable, Teach saw his moment.

"I used to let slip when we were drinking that the English ships would make good targets for us, if only Hornigold changed his mind," Teach reminisced, "but Hornigold is captain, and what the captain says is the word of the ship..."

It didn't take long for the crews to meet and vote out Hornigold as captain and commander of the flotilla. The next most obvious choice was of course Teach.

Blackbeard.

"I never told Hornigold that I helped overthrow him," Teach said inside his head. "But he was too good a captain not to know."

Hornigold, rather than be demoted, took his treasure and sailed off in the *Ranger*, along with one sloop, full of his payment and some loyal crew members. Teach never saw him again. "Such was the life of the citizens of New Providence," he said with a shrug. Teach had heard Hornigold had taken a king's pardon and retired to the good life on shore.

Teach began to realize now that is what he had just tried to do, here in Bath. "How did he do it?" Teach wondered. "How could he be settled on dry land?" A leather shoe scraped the dirt on his porch. He was supposed to be a man of wealth, wearing nice, fancy shoes. In a clean house. He began to miss his long black boots. Part of what had made him Blackbeard.

After Hornigold left, Teach was captain of a decent sized crew, along with Bonnet's men and another sloop. Sitting in drinking establishment, when he heard of another ship passing through the Caribbean. The *Concorde* was an older ship which had passed hands as it had been taken by the French. In a skill equal to pirates in renaming the vessel, they called it *La Concorde* and turned it into a slave trading vessel. Teach knew two things about the ship; it was a large ship still in fairly good shape, and the crew was small, tired, and probably slightly sick. Slavers never carried large crews, and the sheer number of bodies on board, with absolutely no concern over their health, death was almost an hourly visitor to the souls chained in the hold. Sickness would be rampant.

But slavers made gold on their cargo. They would be rich, and would not put up a fight.

But just to be sure...

"That was when I became Blackbeard," he smiled an evil smile.

Dressed as always in his black cloak and long boots, he took his two sloops to the slow moving *La Concorde*. By that time, he had taken to wearing a belt holding three pistols across his chest, all loaded and ready for their dirty work. His cutlass was at his waist. High in his hat he carried a slow wick, used to light off the black powder poured in the cannons' touch holes. He already knew it made a striking visage, but this time, he would use it to the fullest.

"I looked like the Devil from Hell himself," Teach closed his eyes to picture himself, less than a year ago, he realized, as a demon bent on destruction.

As his sloop approached the *La Concorde*, Teach drew one pistol and fired it. The few officers on deck were watching, and saw this striking figure, in black, taller than any man they had seen before, on the bow of a sloop, cannons at the ready. Smoke poured from his head. His beard hung long, tied in ribbons as if to mark the flags of the ships he had taken. In one hand there was his cutlass, longer than most for the big man, curved, glinting in the sun. In the other was the smoking pistol. The simple shot in the air was meant as a question. Are you ready for a fight, or will you give quarter?

The captain of the French ship raised his own pistol and fired. Blackbeard had suspected they would give up with no fight. He didn't think they had any fight in them. But he showed no surprise when the captain signaled back with a shot of his own. "Right. Prepare for boarding."

Then he saw the rest of the crew of *La Concorde* arguing with the captain. Teach had been right. They had no fight in them. He and his two ships' crew boarded with no fight.

The captain was the only one who put up any argument, as he was unwilling to give up the gold they took in payment. But Blackbeard, in simple French and a rather bloody threat, convinced him. The rest of the crew had no desire to test the dark figure. This man was *le diable lui-même.*

The Devil himself.

The gold was a prize, certainly. His men were happy to have the coins. What Teach had wanted was the ship. He put the French crew onto one of his sloops, the smaller of the two, and left the slaves on Bequia, the largest island in the Grenadines. It was a poor choice for a beach, but certainly better than the hold of *La Concorde.*

He immediately renamed the ship. He took his cues from pirate heritage, but with his own style and splash, naming her the *Queen Anne's Revenge.* "Forty guns," Teach remembered people saying. The wide ship would easily hold 40 large cannon, but he only had 36 cannons to spare. He added four by simply shoving wooden barrels out the sides of the ship. The larger number just seemed right. "I could have said it held one hundred and they would have not feared me more."

With the *QAR* and Bonnet's sloop the *Revenge*, now under the more skilled hand of his trusted lieutenant, Thomas Richards, Teach began his real reign of the Caribbean. He took several ships, including the *Great Allen*, a huge, well armed merchantman that put up a serious fight. After its capture, he stranded the crew on and island Saint Vincent, and emptied the hold. Then he burnt the ship in the shallows to the keel.

He stopped and ransacked the *Margaret*, but allowed the captain, Henry Bostock and crew, back aboard after their cargo was removed. Bostock was, if not obliging, at least begrudgingly indifferent. "I had thought of asking him to join me, but he was content with his life as a merchantman. At least he wasn't from Boston."

Teach had, and still did, hate any and all ships from the northern port. If he found a ship from that city, it was quick to fall to the torch. He didn't blame the crew. They were too often recruited by force. But Boston...

Teach hated Boston. They had recently sent out pirate hunter ships, capturing and then hanging pirate crew en masse at the port entrance. Being a pirate, or even just sailor, was a difficult enough career. To die, to be hanged, and then gibbeted and left to feed the seagulls, just to be a sign for others to not take up the career. It was a sick, horrendous way to die. To be left for dead, dried up, forgotten, not a marker for their bodies. He hated, *hated*, Boston, and what they did to pirates.

"As much as people feared me," Teach wondered as he reminisced that day, "I don't think I ever killed a man unless I was in a fight." He had left many for dead, and made no aide to more, but just killed a man, in cold blood, that was just reputation.

"There was that one time, with Israel Hands," he laughed at that, too. At a table while drinking hard with his crew, a drunken Edward Teach drew his two pistols from his belt. He remembered one man, just a swab, but a quick one at that, who jumped up and ran. He knew the game. Israel Hands was drunker, and slower. Teach crossed his arms, pointing the guns under the table, and fired. One hit Hands in the knee, nearly crippling him. He had been of little help since that, Teach regretted. Hands lived in a smaller home nearby in Bath. He still remembered what he said when Hands asked why he did that. "If I don't shoot one of them every once in a while, they will forget who I am."

That had been an especially good time for him. Teach had added several ships to his flotilla, and it quickly became an armada. "A fleet," Teach avoided the Spanish term. He, along with several other captains, and Bonnet, took ships all across the Caribbean, all the while avoiding the growing numbers of military ships that tried and failed to hunt him down.

By May, he was in charge of nine ships of varying size, and well over a thousand men. He was also in charge of the health and well being of his crew. If they were not cared for, fed, and entertained, they would either vote to remove him or leave. His biggest issue was that many of his crew were now sick or wounded from battles and too much close contact. His crew suffered from scurvy, and more suffered from syphilis. He had no medicine, no treatments, and no source for more modern care along the islands of the Caribbean.

But he had a solution for that.

There may be no medicines in the tropical islands, but the big port cities to the north had them. And Charles Town was both close, and easy to access.

He and his ships sailed to the mouth of the harbor, and began to take ships that tried to pass out. Teach had been fortunate to capture a ship, the *Crowley*, traveling to England with several prominent members of Charles Town, including Samuel Wragg, a member of the council of the Carolinas. Dressed in his finest, he and the rest of the passengers were unceremoniously dumped into one of the holds while Blackbeard formulated a plan. He was going to send a message to the town, along with a list of demands. He gathered the captured passengers and informed them together that he wanted a supply of medicines. If he did not get them, all of the captives would die, and he would send their heads to the leaders of Charles Town on sticks.

The group were terrified. These were rich landowners and powerbrokers, not men of the sea. They knew nothing of fighting. One of them, a Mr. Marks, then offered to go ashore with a list of demands. He even offered his own son as hostage to be sacrificed if he did not return.

Ignoring the heartless sacrifice, "I wouldn't kill a boy," Teach grumbled, he took Marks up on the offer.

Marks and two pirates went to the port town in a small rowboat with a list of medicine needed, and a message that if there was no answer in two days, he would kill the prisoners and level the town with his fleet.

The threat was made, in no uncertain terms. So Teach was surprised to wait the two days with no response. He had not asked for gold or treasure. The medicine would truly only be a few hundred pounds in value. Its scarcity on the seas was what made it important. At the end of the second day, a small fishing boat with a thin sailor rowed up to the commodore's big fleet. The poor fisherman, petrified by the sight of so many pirates and so many guns, was shaking at the oars. He informed them that Marks' boat had capsized in the harbor, and that they had not even made it to the town when he was paid to come out to inform the pirates. Blackbeard ordered the man aboard and shored up with rum. It wasn't his fault he had been sent. A little courage would help the man, and he would have a story to tell. He survived drinking with the legendary Blackbeard.

Marks would gather the medicine, ultimately, even though the governor was less than willing to even oblige that small price for these prisoners. But he couldn't find the two pirates who sailed to the port with him. They had enjoyed the town's various watering holes, getting and staying riproaring drunk the entire time they were there.

They only sobered up when Blackbeard sailed in and fired his cannons in a promise of things to come. The two ran as fast as their inebriated feet would carry them to the boat, where they met Marks and his trove of medicine.

"The prisoners had promised to help me attack their own home," Teach thought about the way those men turned so quickly on their own people. "Cowards. Who gives away their own boy as a hostage?" When Charles Town didn't respond, they all feared he would follow through on killing them all, and did anything to save their own heads.

Fortunately for both the prisoners and Blackbeard, the boat appeared, with both the rapidly sobering sailors and a very visible red cloak that Teach had given Marks. It was a sign that a deal had been made.

Teach let the prisoners go. He had no desire to cut their heads off, and he wanted the medicine. But before he sent them back to their home, he stripped them of all their goods, both monetarily, and clothing-wise. Sending the men who were so eager to fight for either side, whichever would help them at the time, only in their undergarments was embarrassment enough. He had what he wanted.

Teach told the prisoners and the captains of the ships he stopped in the blockade that he was headed toward Hispaniola to attack Spanish ships loaded with gold. He knew that there were military ships, men-of-war, loaded with cannon, hunting for him and his fleet, and that they would track him down, sooner or later. He had over a thousand men, but they were trained for piracy, not war. They fought only when the odds were in their favor, and a battle against trained and well armed naval ships and sailors would be decidedly one sided. He had to make a decision.

The governor of North Carolina, Charles Eden, was a man Teach could trust, because the governor would do anything for money. Line his pocket, and Eden would do anything. So when Eden announced a royal pardon for all piracy committed before January 5 of the year, as long as they turned themselves in by September 5, he saw a chance to get out from under the threat of destruction from a well armed British fleet. The actions in Charles Town, in May, would be well after the date of January 5, but again, Eden could be trusted to fix that.

He still had a problem. He had several ships, a large crew, and...

"Bonnet."

Stede Bonnet was still a problem. Demoted from his role as captain, he still owned his ship, and was reaping the benefits of Teach's piratical skill. Teach had a solution, but how to do it.

Instead of heading toward Hispaniola, he announced to his crews that he planned to head toward North Carolina, where they would careen the big ship, the *Queen Anne's Revenge*, to scrape the barnacles from the hull. Over time, especially when sitting in the Charles Town port, barnacles would attach themselves to the ship. Enough of them would dramatically slow the ship, and then damage the wood. Ships had to be regularly careened on a soft beach by sailing into a safe harbor at high tide, then letting the ship settle to one side as the tides let out. The exposed hull could easily be cleaned. But it also meant that the ships and pirates were at the mercy of attack.

North Carolina was a perfect place for that, Teach knew. The entirety of the coast was unoccupied. Not a single town graced the wide sandbar-like islands that lined the coast. The only place where anyone lived was far off Occacoke and the village of Portsmouth, where a few men ran lighters, little ships that could sail the shallow waters of the interior sounds. The rest of the water was nothing but sandy beach and tall grass. Plenty of places to hide.

"That's what I told the crew," he reminisced.

Teach knew the waters well. The sandy interior could change with the whim of a storm, but he was a master at the shallow waters of North Carolina. He knew where the *QAR* could pass, and knew where it couldn't. That, too, was part of his plan.

He confided in Bonnet that he was going to take the pardon from Eden, and then retire. In order to not arouse too much suspicion, he planted the idea in Bonnet's mind that there may be a limit to the royal pardon. While some of his crew thought he suggested Bonnet go first to see if it was safe, Teach really had fooled Bonnet into wanting to go before Teach was able to. "He was easy to deceive," Teach had known.

Then he followed up with the next part of his plan.

Sailing into Beaufort Inlet was a difficult passage of shallow shoals and twisted deep channels. It was a tight fit for the big flagship, but Blackbeard the Pirate could do it with ease, if he wanted to.

"And I didn't want to."

The *QAR* was just too big, with too many crew members, and it was too recognizable. It was his known ship, and everyone would be looking for it, and him. Instead of sailing it into Beaufort Inlet and to the grassy shores near the new little town of Beaufort, he purposefully grounded it onto a wide sandbar, cracking the mast and keel.

It gave Bonnet an chance and excuse to leave, to go get the pardon first. If it was safe and Bonnet was not captured for the actions in Charles Town, Teach, no longer Blackbeard, "I would have to give up the name, for the time," he said, would go and get his own pardon.

He went through the perfunctory actions of trying to save the ship, but he knew it was a lost cause. He loaded the treasure he had, his, many members of the crew's, and especially Bonnet's, and took off toward Bath in a smaller sloop. He abandoned several of Bonnet's crew on an island, taking his more loyal men with him.

By the time Teach had gotten to Bath and gotten his own pardon from Eden, Bonnet had come and gone. Bonnet had rescued the crew, and gone looking for Teach for revenge of taking his portion of the treasures.

Teach looked out over the river again. The water called to him. He knew of the danger. Bonnet had said he would go to the Caribbean and get a commission, but instead he was caught and taken to Charles Town to be imprisoned and readied to be hanged. The pardon didn't entirely protect him, which is why Teach had stayed in Bath. He waited.

But he had waited long enough. He had just gone out on his remaining sloop, renamed the *Adventure*, and taken two sloops in the Delaware Bay. He had told Eden he had "found it," abandoned, derelict, but still with a hold filled with sugar and mead. Eden held an admiralty court, and made it official. The ship had been found, not taken, and belonged to Teach. The sixty barrels of sugar that Eden suddenly acquired certainly helped with the decision.

Now, Teach had thought the time had come. He had spent the last six months as a colorful and respected member of the North Carolina capital. He befriended Eden, the Howard family, which included his mate William Howard, and other wealthy landowners. He had married! But his wild life had not slowed any just because he was no longer on a ship. Rum cost gold, and gold meant work.

Piracy was Teach's career.

The coast called to him.

"Occacoke has always been a friendly place," he said to the wind that blew out over the Pamticough River. Nearby, at the docks, he heard the lines and masts start to sing as the breeze blew through them. He knew Occacoke to be a safe area, but also a great place to spy those fat, slow ships sailing up from the Caribbean, loaded with goods he could sell. He could get more ships, more crew, more rewards.

"Yes, Occacoke would be a good place to start again," he agreed with himself, the only one he had to convince. His crew would be happy to be back out to sea, he knew. He would leave most here, in Bath, and take only twenty or twenty five of them, just enough to handle the ship. There would be no threats in Occacoke, of that he was sure.

He stroked his growing beard. His name would come back. Blackbeard the pirate captain would be remembered again. "I can't let them forget who I am," he said to the winds.

Occacoke would be where he would return. It would be a new beginning. Teach thought back to when he had started into piracy, less than two years ago, in early 1717, when he had received his ship from old Hornigold. No one remembered the once feared pirate Hornigold.

"But they will remember me," Teach said out loud to the river, and to the sound far away before him. This would be the beginning of a new life for him. This time, his reign of piracy would last forever. They would not stop him now.

"On to Occacoke."

The Breakers

A ship isn't even necessary if you want to be a pirate. Coldblooded violence might just be enough.

Nags Head holds many legends, many ghosts, and much history. For a place that was almost completely desolate, empty, until the last hundred years, the town chronicles an amazing number of stories. Somehow, they all intertwine into a cultural epic, a tale that started long ago, and continues to live on today.

But before the stories, there really was nothing. Just a windswept beach, ghost crabs, twisted oaks, and waving sea grasses. So when there is nothing, and the first survivors of shipwrecks wash ashore, they have little in the way of making a better life for themselves. No jobs, certainly no careers, when there is barely even food, water, and shelter. So what choice did they have but to turn to piracy.

Nags Head is famous for its pirates. What made them unique was that they didn't even have ships. The land pirates have a curious history on the island, one which ultimately became attached to the name of the town. Much of what is said about the land pirates and Nags Head is, well, not really made up, not entirely untrue, but certainly embellished and gilded somewhat. But that's what makes the best stories, right?

The first settlements on the Outer Banks were in the late 1600s, in present day Colington Island and nearby Currituck County. Kitty Hawk Village grew at the time as well. But those were chosen destinations. The shipwreck victims, as well as a few nomadic hunters and herders, made their way to the open lands that would become Nags Head.

They would settle on the calm side of the island. The beaches at the time were much too dangerous, with the risk of storms and high waves. The coast was also too far from the tree covered west side of the barrier island, where wood could be harvested for small huts, burned for fire, and animals could be hunted or trapped for food. The sound side, the woods, still had good soil for growing what little seed might take root in the ground. Nothing grew in the sand but salted grass and the ever present ghost crabs, which may have been plentiful but offered no nutritional value to the stranded new inhabitants.

So houses grew, a few at a time, on the west side, sheltered by growing sand dunes that protected the homes from the cold nor'easters that blew in the winter and early spring. But there was little else they could get. It was subsistence at the lowest level. The needs met kept them alive, but only barely. They had to find a way to supplement what they had with things they couldn't normally get.

At the time, shipping was the main mode of transporting goods across the growing colonies, but with the risks of seagoing travel, the cargo ships had to hug the coasts, hoping for safe passage, while using the natural landmarks for navigation.

So, just off the coast, easily visible on the shore or from the tall dunes, ships passed by in each direction, big white sails full, hulls cutting through the water as they carried a bone in their teeth of white water churned to the sides of the bow. All chock full of both riches and necessities. They carried wood, cloth, buttons, gold, rum, whatever they could fit in the hold that would sell for more than what it cost. The merchant sailor was the denizen of the open ocean.

The pirates would hide behind the dunes.

The local residents, as close to natives as they could be, were known as "The Bankers" for their home on the banks, but they would get another name for their action. They became known as "Breakers."

Legend tells that these were the first land pirates of the Outer Banks. They would wait for opportunities, where ships got too close to the coast, then run aground on the shallow sandbars just offshore. Then they would go aboard and pilfer what they could use. It was better when the ships wrecked, cracked open, and spilled their contents to the beach. It usually meant the crew was lost to the sea. But if they had to, the crew could be gotten rid of.

As the saying went, Dead Men Tell No Tales.

While the heyday of pirates at sea was the turn of the 1700s, until Blackbeard met his bloody end, the Breakers didn't have their better days until the turn of the 19th century. The early 1800s saw an increase in sea traffic off of the

Carolina coast, with goods ripe for the picking. If they could only get to them. Thus began a practice that fell into legend, and a name was made for the Breakers.

They could either wait until the ships cracked open on the shoals, or they could bring the ships to them. Legend tells of the Breakers putting a lamp on the neck of an old broken horse, a long suffering descendant of some wild and proud Spanish mustang, no doubt, and walking the poor creature along the dunes at night. Ships in a rough sea would spy the bobbing light in the darkness, and, thinking it was a ship at anchor in a safe port, would sail toward the false harbor. They would then be crashed upon the sandy shoals. The hulls would be stuck good, buried deep in the shallow sandbars. If they were fortunate, the masts did not snap, nor did the keel break and hull spring open, flooding the ship or stranding it. The captain and crew may be able to refloat her at a higher tide by throwing off heavy cargo. That booty, once washed ashore, would be a decent prize for the Breakers.

If the ship was less fortunate, the craft would be broken, and have to be abandoned. Hopefully the crew would make it to shore, and possibly rescue.

But the worst possible outcome would be a stranding, then seeing the small craft of the Breakers, coming from the sandy beaches. Hopes, once afloat for the ship's sailors and officers, would soon be as dashed as the ship was. The people aboard just were of no value to the Breakers.

Houses were built of the timber from many shipwrecks on the Outer Banks. It is suspected that under many of the oldest houses in Nags Head there still are pieces of the sturdy oak that was used in building many of the ships from hundreds of years ago. And as likely many of those houses were also decorated with items "found" inside those ships.

For that is part of the legacy of Nags Head; an old nag, with a lamp around its drooping neck, endlessly plodding across the rolling sand hills in the middle of the night, is where, it is alleged, that the name Nags Head came from.

But of course, so much of this just just legend, right? The name, the Breakers, ships' crews forced to walk the plank, it can't be true, can it?

Nags Head most likely did not get its name from a poor horse that walked the dunes, let alone tromped up and down Jockey's Ridge back in the 1800s. No horse, no matter how beaten down, would tolerate a candle burning just under her neck. The story is apocryphal, and the name Nags Head was likely applied to the land by a poor English sailor or a colonist who saw the rugged shore as similar to a similarly named place on the English coast.

And, while it was certainly tradition, an expected behavior, to take whatever came from the ocean as their own, an aquatic finders keepers game played by the local Bankers, they wouldn't really board ships and force the crews to a watery death, or worse.

Would they?

One story says otherwise.

By the 1850s, the Outer Banks and Nags Head had become a tourist mecca. It may be hard to believe, but that early on, Nags Head was a destination. It was a wonderful summer respite for the plantation owners of Edenton and other towns inland. They would load up their family, servants and slaves, even the family dog, and move everyone to simple homes built on the same soundside that the old native Bankers called home just a few decades before. Of course, these wealthy well dressed people would have nothing to do with the lowly Bankers, so poor they barely scraped through, by selling seafood caught in the sound for the tourists' evening meals. The fancy houses reached out into the sound waters to meet the mailboats, the delivery boats from Elizabeth City, and the occasional visitor from nearby Roanoke Island.

The inland tourists loved Nags Head. It was windy, but sunny, and usually ten degrees cooler than the stifling heat inland. There the air was thick, humid, and full of mosquitoes. On the Outer Banks, the wind blew sweetly, keeping the insects at bay, for the most part.

As families continued to come down, staying for the entire summer of twelve weeks, not just one, they began to want more decent accommodations than the leaky shacks that the had thrown up years ago.

In the 1860s, a doctor from Elizabeth City, William Poole, purchased twelve lots of land on the beach side of Nags Head, because his wife wanted to be closer to the ocean, and not have to walk in the deep sand in her shoes and dress, nor did she enjoy the rutted ride of a horse drawn carriage. It would take time, especially as the Civil War raged, but by the late 1860s, he built her a house.

And since it was the first house on the beach, ever, and he didn't want his wife to be lonely, he sold the other lots to all their friends, so they could build there, too.

Even as this initial growth of tourism and part time residents grew in Nags Head, most of the island residents were near dirt poor. They lived a subsistence life, gleaning what they could from the nearby forest floor that would later become Nags Head Woods. They had no ability to quickly and regularly gain access to the tinctures and salves that could ease even the most basic of wounds. While the coast may be a great place to grow old, at the time, sick people did not live long on the Outer Banks.

Since Dr. Poole was a regular resident to the beach, he was often called upon in his professional capacity. This time he was asked to tend to a very old woman who was obviously not long for the earth. He was asked if there was anything he could do to ease her pain.

So he visited, and did what he could, but he informed the family that she had little time left. She should simply be made as comfortable and stress free as possible. The poor Banker family, appreciative of the care Dr. Poole had given her, could not pay even a penny for his services.

But Dr. Poole had noticed that, even in the sad confines of the little Banker hut, there was a rather beautiful portrait of a woman, who bore no likeness to the family. He asked the old lady about the portrait as a way to engage her to distraction.

The old woman, seeming to drift in and out of consciousness and lucidity, became more coherent at the mention of the portrait. And she began her tale.

She explained that her family were the descendants of Breakers, the land pirates of Nags Head. She told the stories of how ships would become stranded, and how her father and others like him would go out to the shore and take what they could from the broken shipwrecks.

Dr. Poole, like most living on the islands at the time, knew the tales of the Breakers, but he suspected they were

mostly legends, with very little to back up the claims with real evidence or documented history. But here was a real and true descendant of one of the very land pirates. And she told her story of how she had come to own the portrait.

The portrait was from a ship they had captured and stripped of all goods. A ship had been lured to the shallows where it was stranded and its masts snapped. What few crew had survived the recent storm were badly injured from the wreck, and they were all quickly dispatched. There was only one passenger, a rather regal woman, dressed in white, a fancy dress better meant for a gala than a gale, who held her head high and proud, even at the threats of the Breakers.

She was going to be taken ashore and held captive, possibly, or maybe she was going to receive care, as she did not look well. Whatever the actions of the Breakers were that they planned were laid asunder when instead the beautiful woman stepped over the gunwale and into the roiling ocean. The dress that was so beautiful on her quickly became an anchor. The flowing layers soaked in salt water, weighting her down. The woman made no attempt to swim, to escape to the shore, to even save her own life, but instead sank to the sandy bottom of the ocean. Lost to the tides.

The portrait was that of the woman who threw herself over the side of the ship to keep her from being yet another treasure for the Breakers.

Dr. Poole thought the story was remarkable. But he had no reason to doubt it. How else would these poor Bankers have ever gotten such a well made painting. Though who was she? It was a mystery.

The family thanked Dr. Poole for the care and comfort, and the medicine he provided. They felt bad they had nothing to pay him with, and the old lady's son offered him the portrait in payment instead. It did them no good, and he had no attachment to the picture. Dr. Poole seemed more enamoured of it than they would ever be, and he could have it if he wanted.

Dr. Poole, gracious for the gift, and not wanting to insult them, took the portrait with a great deal of thanks. He so valued the picture that he took it home to Elizabeth City rather than leave it to the elements at Nags Head.

The entirety of this story could be written up to fantasy, or legend, just a tale told by islanders as a fun little story. But there is, of course, more to the legend.

At the end of 1812, Theodosia Burr-Alston boarded the fast schooner *Patriot* to see her father, Aaron Burr, the former Vice President of the United States, and later to be famous for the murder of Alexander Hamilton in a duel. Theodosia had not seen her father in over five years. She had lost her son at a young age, and probably suffered from cancer at the time. Her husband put her on the *Patriot* with express directions to the captain to care for her at all costs. He probably knew she would not come back to his home in South Carolina.

He would be correct, but not for reasons he knew.

The ship would sail off on New Years Eve, December 31, 1812, and would never be seen again.

There were numerous unsubstantiated rumors as to the loss of the ship, and what happened to Theodosia, including being taken by pirates off of Southport, NC.

What is known is that Theodosia boarded the *Patriot* with a gift for her father, a painting of her to be presented when they next met.

And that the portrait that Dr. Poole received bears a striking resemblance to Theodosia.

No one really knows what happened to Theodosia and the ship she sailed upon, nor can they even be sure it made it all the way to the Outer Banks. Some suspect a slightly more mundane tale, where the ship was taken by British privateers and burned or hobbled, and the crew killed, somewhere far to the south. The remains of the hull may have just drifted up to Nags Head before finally making landfall. The Breakers, finding the portrait, took it as a souvenir, along with more useful stuff, in what was left.

But then, it may be as likely that poor Theodosia met a watery end just offshore of present day Jockey's Ridge, just one of many victims of the merciless Breakers, the land pirates of Nags Head.

Stede Bonnet

He called himself a gentleman pirate, but the words did not match with his deeds.

Piracy as a legend has run the gamut, nautically, over the centuries since the late 1600s. A pirate could be a hero, when seen in the right light. Sir Francis Drake is a legend in history and in schoolbooks as the first Englishman to sail around the world. He is considered nothing less than a great navigator and skilled captain by the British.

Ask the Spanish at the time, however, and he was nothing but a dirty murdering filthy pirate.

That's the way it was, and still is, with pirates. A privateer was a hero to one nation, a hired mercenary to that nation's enemies.

A pirate was even worse. They had no loyalty to anyone except themselves. "A merry life and a short one," a quote that was attributed to the great pirate Benjamin Hornigold, may well sum up the beliefs of all pirates of that golden age. While the governments and merchant ships generally saw them as a scourge upon the seas, most people had a more romantic view of pirates. They saw the rogue buccaneers as being a Robin Hood of the seas, taking from wealthy merchants who gave little back, but demanded backbreaking work from the field to the dock to the ship. Piracy was seen as, if not glamorous, at least more rewarding than a sad and long life of servitude.

Perhaps this is what called Stede Bonnet out of his life of comfort as a plantation owner in Barbados.

Bonnet was born on the island to an already wealthy family that owned 400 acres of land. He served in the militia there, retiring as a major. However, being in the army when living on an island meant he probably saw little to no fighting. He certainly spent no time on any ship other than as the occasional passenger.

So it certainly was a strange turn of events when he up and turned pirate from a life on land.

Some speculation say it was a melange of tragedy that drove him slightly mad. He had been married in 1709, had four children, and was tiring of his life as a husband and father. One son died young, which may have added to his melancholy. No one really knows if it was a tiring and bothersome wife, the loss of a child, the tiring responsibilities of an estate, or just the fancy of being a pirate that drove him from one life to another. It very well may have been all of it. But Stede Bonnet, wealthy, respected, successful that he was, decided to fly the black flag.

Strangely, he not only bought his ship, while most pirates stole or commandeered theirs, he actually had it built, saying he was going to use it for merchant trade throughout the islands of the Caribbean. He may have wanted to have some form of denial of his intentions while at his home. Declaring to be a professional pirate was something that just was not done in his social circles.

Considering he had his ship outfitted with ten cannon and overtly made a point to hire sailors with the intention of pirating, he did little else to hide his plans. He had his ship built and crewed, named it the *Revenge*, a not so clever nor unique name toward piracy, and slunk off in the middle of the night.

It was clear in the first moments that Bonnet knew nothing about piracy. He had no experience captaining a ship. He leaned upon the more experienced quartermaster and mates he had hired to actually run the ship. He mostly wanted the thrill and fun of being at sea, away from rules and responsibility. He still dressed well, in his riches and finery, which were poor clothing choices aboard a sailing vessel. But it did earn him a nickname that would later have some gallows humor. Stede Bonnet, *The Gentleman Pirate*.

In the spring of 1717, Bonnet began his sail from Barbados toward the Virginia colony, where he stalked the

Chesapeake Bay, taking four ships, including the *Turbes*. Most ships he merely stripped of their valuable goods, but the *Turbes* he burned. It was Barbadian sailing vessel, so it was suspected he didn't want anyone from the ship ever getting back to the Caribbean home island to tell of his treacherous exploits. He took his prisoners to Gardiner's Island in New York to drop them. He did not find the area particularly conducive to piracy, so he returned to the Carolinas and more fertile, and safer, hunting grounds.

There he took more ships, including another Barbadian sloop, which he used for careening his *Revenge* to clean the hull. He then again burned the Barbadian craft to hide his new career. From there it was back to the Caribbean, on to Nassau and the free pirate town of New Providence, a floating city of transient pirates where they could trade and restock their ships in relative safety.

Unfortunately for Bonnet, on the way he discovered the greater lack of safety when he fought with a Spanish Man-o-War. Against the more formidable warship, Bonnet was seriously wounded, and the ship and crew were fortunate to escape with their lives. He would limp into New Providence an injured man.

Good fortune would shine upon the crew of Bonnet's *Revenge*. Stede Bonnet himself may have felt different about his luck if he knew what was to come, but at the time, he was happy with whom he crossed paths. There in New Providence he met both the highly successful pirate Benjamin Hornigold, and Hornigold's protege, Edward Teach. Teach would quickly go on to become infamous as the notorious pirate Blackbeard.

It seemed strange to many, but Teach, the skilled and somewhat mad captain became close friends with the fancy high society Bonnet. Bonnet, Hornigold, and Teach decided to sail together as a fleet. Bonnet probably saw the success of the two more well known pirates and thought it best to join forces.

Or, it may have been that fortune favored Blackbeard.

Bonnet's skill and success in piracy had more to do with his crew's skills than his as a captain. Again, he had never commanded a ship, nor crew, but did hire a large number of well seasoned pirates when he put out of Barbados six months earlier. He made rather strange decisions as a captain. He was notoriously brutal with both his captives and with his crew. Most pirate captains were elected, and any abuse would quickly lead to a mutiny by vote. But Bonnet had hired his crew, paying them a salary instead of a cut of the loot, which was odd for a pirate ship. He was also known to actively injure or kill captives. He may have even made prisoners walk the plank. That colorful execution is often threatened in pirate lore and legend, but it was not done in real life. Pirates were just the other side of the coin from a sailor. Many on the receiving end of a pirate boarding would soon join the pirates in their own fight. Pirates knew that a good bit of color, especially in Blackbeard's case, could scare a crew into surrender, but it was almost always bluster, with no bloodshed on the merchant ships that didn't want to put up a fight.

Bonnet was the exception to that rule. He seemed to enjoy the violence and threats. This may have had something to do with his significant change in mental state when he first went a-pirating. But no matter the reason, even his crew knew, this man was no captain.

The crew of Bonnet's *Revenge,* possibly with the surreptitious suggestion from Blackbeard during a drinking spree in New Providence, asked for Teach to take over the *Revenge,* while Bonnet was placed aboard Teach's sloop to recover more fully from his injuries. With little in the way of argument against both two pirate captains and a violent crew who could easily get rid of Bonnet, the Gentleman Pirate removed himself to Teach's sloop, where he took little part in any future actions while he recovered from his injuries.

Once healed, Bonnet decided to take back his ship, and he and Blackbeard parted. Bonnet did little to endear himself to his crew, who lusted for the success they had under Blackbeard. When Bonnet chased the huge merchant ship *Protestant Caesar* and lost it without a fight, they had had enough. The next time they encountered Blackbeard, they nearly demanded he take over the *Revenge.*

By this time Teach, now well known by his *nom de guerre* of Blackbeard, had taken the ship *La Concorde,* and renamed it *Queen Anne's Revenge,* making it his flagship. Teach, probably with a bit of prodding by cutlass, insisted that Bonnet, a man more used to wealth and leisure, stay aboard his large ship, while the rough Blackbeard captain the *Revenge.* While Teach would insist that Bonnet was his guest, with nowhere else to go on an open sea, and unwelcome even on his own ship, Bonnet was effectively a prisoner. He confided to a few of his loyal crew that he would retire from piracy if he could escape to Spain.

Blackbeard quickly took control of the fleet, earning fortune and fame. He placed his trusted and skilled lieutenant Thomas Richards in charge of the *Revenge*, and used his fleet to hold Charles Town in the colony of South Carolina under siege for medicine his crew desperately needed. Blackbeard took several ships and crews, and gained a large amount of valuable treasured cargo. Bonnet was a spectator for the entire time that Blackbeard wrote his name into history.

At that time, the Golden Age of Piracy was both at its height and at its end. Pirates were too much of a threat. The colonial governors were sending out skilled captains on heavily armed ships to combat the pirates in their waterlogged sloops. And the crown found their own ways of ending the pirate menace. If caught, a pirate's life would end with a short drop on a scratchy rope. Their bodies would then be displayed as a warning, picked clean over the years by crows and gulls. A pirate's life may be merry, but his death was short, and ugly.

So when Governor Charles Eden of North Carolina offered a pardon for all pirates who surrendered by September 5, 1718, for all crimes committed before January 5th, Blackbeard and Bonnet decided to head toward North Carolina to take the trusted, or easily bribed, Eden up on his offer.

It was a curious set of events, not entirely well documented, that happened next. Bonnet and Teach sailed to present day Topsail Island, with the intention to go take the pardon. Blackbeard was a skilled, experienced sailor who knew the shifting shoals of North Carolina, especially the inlets to the capital Bath town, yet he somehow ran aground with his flagship, *Queen Anne's Revenge*. He convinced Bonnet to go ahead first, even though Teach wondered if the offer of pardon was legitimate. Bonnet went ahead to get his pardon, possibly with the promise that he would get back his ship again, and be free of the dreaded Blackbeard.

While Bonnet went inland and received his pardon, Teach scuttled the wrecked *QAR*, and unloaded the *Revenge*, while stranding several of Bonnet's crew. He then went to Bath to receive his own pardon from Eden. Bonnet had stayed long enough to get permission to sail to St. Thomas where he could get a privateering license. When Bonnet left Bath, Teach arrived.

By the time Bonnet made it back to Topsail, Blackbeard was long gone, along with their booty. Bonnet rescued his crew and began to repair his ravaged *Revenge*.

After outfitting the ship with food and supplies, he gave chase after the double crossing Blackbeard, but could not find him to exact his revenge. But without food and gear, Bonnet resorted back to piracy to get what he needed. He changed his name to Captain Thomas and renamed his ship the *Royal James*. (It is speculated that many pirates turned against England when the Stuart family, including King James, was usurped by the House of Hanover and King

George I. Thus the ship's name.) Bonnet, now Thomas, took several ships in the Delaware Bay.

But the attacks and sailing took their toll on the *Royal James*, now not so royal. She was leaking, barnacle encrusted, and in need of careening somewhere safe. Bonnet decided to take his ship into the Cape Fear, a place of deep water but shallow banks, a great place to hide from hunting warships and dangerous armed sailors.

All this time, more and more colonies grew weary of the pirate attacks. South Carolina colonial governor Robert Johnson ordered a force to seek out pirates, hunt them down, and bring them in to Charles Town, where they would be tried, and then hanged until they all were dead, dead, dead.

Colonel William Rhett was employed along with two sloops and seventy men for a campaign to hunt down every dreaded pirate they could find. They had almost immediately heard of a pirate ship careened in the Cape Fear River in nearby North Carolina. That would be a good target of opportunity.

But the prize they sought was not Bonnet, who was more an irritant than a threat. The South Carolinians wanted the infamous Charles Vane. He had recently plundered several vessels just off of the harbor. One skipper reported hearing Vane say he planned to go south, where he would make repairs. Rhett took off after the pirate, but only too late did he learn that Vane had deceived them. He had purposefully said his statement within earshot of the poor skipper in hopes he would tell any pursuers.

So, with time not on his side, Rhett decided to head back toward the ship in the Cape Fear. It very well could be Vane, who likely did need to make repairs.

Rhett sailed into the Cape Fear in September of 1718, hopeful of finding an accommodating target. He had both fortune and misfortune. Such were the ways of the tides when sailing. Unfamiliar with the uncharted river, for no settlement was built there at the time, Rhett's ships ran aground on the sandbars at the mouth of the river.

But in the misfortune, there was fortune, and misfortune again. Though they had been stranded, they now saw their enemy. The *Royal James* was careened on a sandbar, almost within cannon and musket range.

When the tide changed enough to refloat, both groups began the battle. With broadsides fired by both opponents, all the ships and crews took terrible damage.

Rhett commanded two ships, the *Sea Nymph* and the *Henry*. While he tried to manoeuvre the two into an attack position, and Bonnet tried to outwit Rhett, all the ships again became stranded in shallow waters. But this time, misfortune again struck Rhett. The *Sea Nymph* was stranded too far to be engaged in the fight, and the *Henry* listed its open deck toward Bonnet's *Royal James*. Bonnet, stranded, but with his keel facing Rhett's attacks, was able to fire mercilessly at Rhett's ship. Only through relentless fire under the threat of imminent death at the hands of the pirates, Rhett and his men began to fire cannonballs through the hull of the *Royal James*.

Fortune again raised her hand, this time raising the water enough that the *Henry* was freed from the sandbar, and Rhett was able to manoeuvre the ship to bear down on the vulnerable side of Bonnet's *Royal James*. Bonnet threatened to blow up the ship and all aboard rather than surrender. He pulled his pistols and threatened his own crew that he would blow the brains out of anyone who did not fight to the death.

His threats fell on deaf and fearful ears. The pirates decided to take their chances with a court rather than at the end of a cutlass or cannon. While the men argued, someone ran up a flag of surrender, and the crew of the *Royal James* were ultimately forced to give up.

Captain Thomas, now discovered to be the violent Gentleman Pirate Stede Bonnet, was taken back to South Carolina for trial. His end of piracy would come on an empty river mouth in North Carolina.

Bonnet would hope to escape the gallows in South Carolina, through conniving, with his pardon, or by appealing to his social equals in hopes they would forgive him. When that did not work, and his execution set, bribery was tried. As guards turned a blind eye, he and another pirate attempted their escape. It had been well planned, with a sailing boat prepared for them to make their way back to North Carolina.

But again, fortune prevailed. A wind blew against them, sending them to nearby Sullivan's Island, where they were quickly recaptured.

Bonnet, once the wealthy, fancy dressed Gentleman Pirate, once the dreaded violent captain, skilled in depravity, now became a mere shell of himself, a continual whimpering soul, begging for a last chance not to swing from the hangman's noose. It was all for naught. On December 10, 1718, he would fall from a cart while tied to a rope, and hang until he was indeed dead.

Not even the pauper's field would be good enough for the pirate Bonnet. He was buried in the marsh with no marker for his body. He would outlive his more infamous one time partner Blackbeard by only eighteen days.

The Flaming Ship Of Ocracoke

A ghost story is just that, a story. But they often have a flame of truth in their mystery and history.

Pirates and pirate stories are notorious for being filled with half-truths, exaggerations, and bald lies. A good legend never hurt the bad reputation of a pirate captain and crew. Just ask Blackbeard.

So a good ghost story may be nothing more than that, a story, something made up to keep the kids awake or scare a few of the landlubbers at a late night campfire on the beach.

But then, those stories can be even better if they turn out to be true. Mixing a good ghost story with a good bloody pirate tale, and tossing in a salt water bucketful of historical truth gives us the Flaming Ship Of Ocracoke.

The story begins not in quiet little Ocracoke Village, but far, far away, in what is now known as Germany, in a group of territories known as the Palatinate, which was located in the Rhine area around Germany and Switzerland. The lands were beautiful tree covered rolling hills and humid cool valleys, all excellent for vineyards, as well as a peaceful home to Protestant allies to the new king and queen of

111

England, William and Mary. It also was a place of horrible war, where the Palatines were caught in the middle of huge fights not of their making. The Palatines found themselves refugees, trekking to England, where their skills were unwelcome because their talents put many English tradesmen out of work.

When a Swiss Palatine baron, Cristoph von Graffnreid, suggested that he be given money to hire a ship and take a group of Palatines to the New World, the English Parliament readily agreed.

Hiring a ship and crew was not difficult. There were many to choose from. Hiring a good, trustworthy crew, that was different. The wealthy Palatines may have had the money, but their green meadows and landlocked valleys from a far distant country meant they had little practice in judging the trustworthiness of a captain and sailors. They decided a simple deception would be best.

The wealthy refugees chose to dress in rags, hiding their finery and money with colonial supplies, so as to look undesirable for robbery. They loaded their goods aboard their hired ship, and set out to meet other colonists at a Swiss settlement somewhere in the Carolinas. It was named after their homeland capital, Berne, Switzerland, with the title New Berne. There they hoped to apply their skills and settle down in peace, far away from the struggles of their war ravaged home.

The trip went without incident. For the six week crossing, the Palatines did their best to hide from the crew, which they quickly realized were ruthless and dangerous.

Many had obviously been pirates, and would without thought rob the Palatines of their gold if they only knew about it. But the Palatines kept their mouths closed, only enquiring on occasion of their location and time to the New World.

Finally, after the six week passage, the Palatines were rewarded with the sight of land. They had come upon the opening to the shallow sound behind Ocracoke and Portsmouth Island. The captain explained that the ship could not pass through the inlet; it was far too narrow a channel, with ever shifting bars hidden just below the water. No, the Palatines would have to wait for lighters, smaller craft to come out to them from Portsmouth Island, to unload both the colonists and their goods. They would be taken onto the shallow draft schooners with skilled local captains who could navigate the sounds and waters all the way to New Berne.

The Palatines were delighted! Their salvation, a new world, *the* New World, awaited them. In their joy, some spoke too loudly of the treasure they bore with them. A scoundrel swab overheard the Palatines discussing their treasured wealth.

He quickly made his way to the quartermaster, then to the captain. All of the crew were pirates, up to the officers and captain himself. It was quickly agreed. They would not allow the Palatines to leave yet, and in the middle of the night, the pirate crew would take the hidden treasure.

And no Palatine would ever tell of it.

So it seemed odd to both the Palatines and to the O'cockers on board the small ships that came up to relieve the big vessel of its passengers when the captain waved them off. He called out to them, saying they would anchor just offshore, and that the ships should come back tomorrow.

The Palatines did not understand why they didn't leave immediately, but being landlubbers, they took the captain at his word.

That night, as the Palatines slept, the crew went below and murdered every soul in the group of colonists. Every man, woman, and child was killed silently in their bunks, their throats cut by the jagged dull blades of a remorseless pirate. Then, they cracked open the supplies the Palatines brought, and divided up the immense treasures that had been brought on the trip.

As a final act of treachery, the captain and crew, laden down with the weight of fine clothes and jewelry, lowered themselves into the two dinghies, and set fire to the worm eaten ship, filled now only with the dead.

As they rowed their way from the burning ship in the middle of the night, the light of the fire alerted some of the locals on the island, but all they could do was watch. There was no stopping a fire at sea, not until the ocean poured in and drowned the ship, sending it to the depths.

The pirate crew watched as well, thinking they had escaped with their riches easily. It was only a few moments, though, that they noticed something very strange. The ship, while it burned, was not consumed. The sails snapped from the lines and unfurled, sending the ship forward in a hot, brimstone soaked breeze. The ship began to follow the crew in their tenders, then it started to gain on them.

The pirates redoubled their efforts, putting their backs into the oars. But drunken sailors overloaded with ill-gotten gold were no match for a ship run by vengeful wraiths. As the ship got closer, the pirates could even hear a wail as the dead Palatines called out in pain and anguish at what had happened to them. They had been so close, the  families ready to start anew, to finally find peace, and the only peace they found was at the end of a knife.

The ship gathered speed as it overtook the closer dinghy. The great keel crashed into the wooden rowboat. It was no contest between the great burning ship and the little tender. The rowboat was split in two, with the benches, the gunwales, all crashed to splinters. The pirates were thrown into a merciless cold September ocean. Their treasures that they had counted and cherished only moments before now weighed them down as they were pulled to the bottom. The sea floor was shallow there, but much too deep for a man. They would be pinned to the sandy sea floor, eyes open as they drowned, staring up at the dimming stars and the orange flames of their own ship.

Then the ship turned to the other tender.

Seeing what had happened, and able to hear the laments of the dead as they burned forever on the ship, the rest of the pirates became manic. Some rowed compulsively, the oars coming out of the oarlocks with every stroke. Others so feared for their lives at the approaching hull that they simply dove overboard, only to be pulled down into the waves.

The bow hit the second tender at even greater speed. It sent the pirates flying into the darkness. Many did not drown but were broken by the keel. Their bodies were torn by the barnacle encrusted hull. The captain was run through and drowned in the ship's wake.

Only two of the pirates survived the onslaught. They washed ashore, beaten by the waves, soaked and sputtering as they had breathed in too much salt water. When the locals pulled them to dry sand, they immediately confessed their crimes, and then expired right on the shore.

The Ocracokers were horrified. They had a meager existence, and had long been known to tolerate a bit of piracy, but murdering people in their sleep was beyond the pale. The two bodies were seen as monsters, and left to let the ocean take them.

Then they stared out at the burning ship. Surely what the two dying men said could not be true. The ship would soon consume itself and sink. They were sure of it. They watched, waiting for the flames to either engulf the decks or be extinguished. Neither would happen.

The ship continued to sail, powered by an otherworldy wind. As it got closer to the shore, the locals on the beach could hear the eerie and horrific wail of the dead from within the hull. The plaintive call was both tragic and sad, as if lamenting that they would never reach the shore to which they had come so near. The ship first headed south, toward the opening of Ocracoke Inlet, then turned, defying the winds that blew, and headed northeast. First the wailing disappeared, carried away in the salty ether to a netherworld. Then the ship itself finally passed into the darkness, its light fading to obscurity.

It is said by long time locals that ship reappears on the first new moon of the month of September. A brightening glow crests over the horizon, a ship of fire that somehow does not burn up. It glows orange. The flames lick at the sails and race up the lines, but the ship never is consumed. As it gets closer, the wails of the damned are heard over the wind. The ship sails south, then turns back north, to disappear for another year. The ghosts of the Palatines are forever in a journey to find their way to their new home, so close, but ever so far.

Now, the Flaming Ship of Ocracoke is a great story, full of weird supernatural events, pirates, and murder. But it surely isn't real, is it?

Well...

Christoph von Graffnreid was a real Swiss baron, but not so much a fancy man of high noble blood. He mostly took the job of leading the Palatines to the New World in order to make some money and pay off his debts he still had in Switzerland. He really did take a shipload of Palatine refugees to North Carolina to start the colony of New Bern.

Now, this is where history and the spooky tale of the flaming ship take differing tacks. Von Graffnreid's ship actually was attacked by pirates; French privateers stopped the ship and took everything the colonists had, leaving them only the clothes on their backs. Christoph von Graffnreid would have to go back to England for more supplies and more clothes.

It was a good thing he went back for a change, too.

Von Graffnreid and his colonists settled New Bern on an old abandoned Tuscarora village. The Tuscarora were not happy with the Europeans settling in their land. So when von Graffnreid was scouting the land with fellow colonist/explorer John Lawson, the two were captured by the Tuscarora. They planned to kill the two, but were afraid of the repercussions of killing von Graffnreid. Due to his fancy clothes he had brought back, they assumed he was the colonial governor, and the retribution would be too great.

John Lawson was not as well dressed, nor as lucky.

Christoph von Graffnreid survived a pirate attack and capture by the natives in North Carolina to return to Bern, "old" Bern, Switzerland, to become a low level public official and live his life out in obscurity.

He should have become a storyteller.

Mad Mag

Seeking treasure is a greedy task. Taking another's joy from them can have some dire consequences.

Pirates steal gold, right? Treasure, jewels, gold and silver in wonderfully ornate chests that are locked and sealed. They bury the treasure and make a map to find it, and X marks the spot.

That's the story we all were told as kids, and that's the one we tell to this day. As kids we knew, we just *knew*, that Blackbeard's gold was buried in our backyard or just under our beach towel; all we had to do was dig a little, and we would be rich beyond our wildest dreams.

As long as the treasure wasn't cursed, of course. We all knew that, too. Pirate gold, the ill-gotten booty stained crimson with the blood of innocent sailors and merchants who fought in vain to save their hard earned coins, was always cursed. No good came of taking another's treasure. Well, we kids weren't taking. We were recovering. And, finders, keepers.

The only problem with all that is that pirates sometimes didn't just take gold and jewels. They may not even be considered pirates, in the strictest definition of the term. But what else do you call a sailing captain who takes something that isn't his and sails away to keep it? Pirate is as good a name as any other.

Then, there is that curse...

No one thinks about the curse. Until it is too late.

John Simon Howard was not a pirate. He was an Ocracoke native and skipper of a schooner that sailed the Atlantic waters all the way up into Maine. It may have been cold and windy up there, but the far north coast brought with it trading goods that just couldn't be found in little Ocracoke.

John Simon also found something else, or in this case, someone else that he knew he couldn't find anywhere else.

John Simon Howard put in to Rockport Harbor in Maine in 1896, ostensibly to do what sailors do, make trade, resupply, and possibly find a watering hole with which to commune with some local spirits, from a bottle, that is. While there, he discovered that Rockport had a rather cherished treasure, in the form of Margaret Eaton.

Margaret was beautiful, strikingly so, with long blonde curls, a cherubic face with pearl white skin, bright, vibrant eyes, and a dainty figure. She was an accomplished pianist, and had an angel's voice, it was said. That she had accomplished all this and more, with numerous talents at her hands, was surprising enough. What made her even more remarkable was that she was only fifteen years old.

John Sime, at twenty years older than the girl, was smitten. He saw no other choice than to either make her swoon for him, or just go ahead and kidnap the girl.

He likely chose the latter, though no one really can be sure.

He did certainly put her on his schooner and make way back to Ocracoke, marrying her during the journey. Since he was the captain, and the groom, there was no one to argue against the two being together, it seemed.

John Sime brought Margaret Eaton, now Margaret Howard, back to his home in Ocracoke. Far away from her home, and with neither a boat nor a road to make passage back to Maine, there she realized she would remain.

This would be the beginning of her passing from beautiful Margaret into Mad Mag.

Remember, if you steal another's treasure, you are likely to get a curse along with it.

John Sime took young Maggie to their new house, and had her put up shop as a wife to him. While John Sime may have been infatuated with her, he still was a sea captain, and had to put out to the ocean regularly. So poor Maggie was first kidnapped and forcibly married to an older man who seemed like he was madly infatuated with her, only to have her cast ashore and him leave for days and weeks on end. It may have been a blessing for her; it may have become a blessing for him not to be around her.

And, still, there's that curse.

Maggie Eaton Howard began to drift toward madness over the next twenty years of marriage to John Sime. While he may have been in love with her, she certainly was not with him, at least by her actions. One day, perhaps being tired of a steady diet of seafood and occasional vegetables, she killed and cooked the pet cat for John Sime. The poor mouser never stood a chance against Maggie and her deteriorating mind.

She would do lots of rather crazy things, which would earn her the nickname "Mad Mag," a sobriquet that would follow her to the grave, and beyond. She likely suffered from self-harm, something that wasn't diagnosed in the early twentieth century, and certainly not on an isolated island like Ocracoke. Mad Mag had two notable injuries that she did to herself. She burned her forehead with an iron to brand herself. And she chopped off her own big toe with a meat cleaver. It's possible that she either wanted to prove within herself that she could tolerate the pain she was suffering or she thought it might get attention. Often the self injury is a form of coping mechanism for those who suffer from self-harm. While people may have been paying attention, they just didn't do anything about it for her.

At least, not until John Sime finally up and left her by dying. When John Simon Howard died in 1923, the locals felt sorry for Mad Mag, and built her a small house on Paddy's Hollow, a low rise of a sand dunes just off of old Howard Street. It was near a footpath that ran from the village to the beach. It may have been meant to be convenient to poor Mag, but the path may have driven her even more mad.

Locals found it easier to just walk up along her porch as they passed by, and the kids enjoyed tormenting the poor widow, alone in a land not her home while only in her forties. They would bang on the walls and doors, then run away, while Maggie screeched at them.

Mad Mag took to wearing her nightgown all the time, often wandering the streets, her hair now grown long and gray from the stress. She would be seen, standing alone, wild, yelling, maddened by ghosts that only she could see, or perhaps walking up and down the dusty roads in her gown and twisted salted hair, blown wild by the ocean winds.

If she was going to curse John Sime and Ocracoke for bringing her there, it was going to be a hell of a good one.

So, that curse...

When a pirate steals gold that is cursed, covered in blood and death, there is usually only one way to end the curse. That is by returning the treasure to its rightful place. With John Sime long dead, he was not going to be able to do that. And soon Margaret "Mad Mag" Eaton Howard would pass on, too. And then there would be no way to return the cursed gold coin that once was the young and beautiful Margaret Eaton.

Which meant the curse was just going to stay, and they might as well live with it.

Soon after Mad Mag died, people began seeing and hearing her ghost appear in the Howard family cemetery. She is easily recognized, as she wears the same faded dress, a creamy, dusty white gray. Her hair is as long and wild as when she was alive. She wears a local necklace, a simple creation of seashells strung on twine. She is known to stand at the graves and shriek, an otherworldly banshee call. Her screams are possibly primal frustrations of having to be forever interred but never at rest in a land that was not her own.

People have even seen her in the twilight as an old woman who walks the dusty roads as the sun sets. Her feet are unaffected by the hot clay road, or the rocks and sharp oyster shells that layer the old dirt streets, as she lightly floats, never leaving a footprint. She has been seen, but not heard. People have spoken to her, mistaking her for an old lady out for a stroll, until they notice she does not respond. She seems like she never notices anyone or anything, as she makes her way into the darkness.

So be careful when you look for treasure, or be prepared to take the bad with the good. The moral of this story is, don't take who is not yours.

Pirates Of The Carolina Coast

North Carolina is still a wild place along the coast, even today. In the Golden Age of Piracy, it was still a natural land, and with the rolling hills and growing grass, it was a great place for pirates to hide, and then to fall.

Not every pirate made a name for themselves that would go down in history. When asked what pirates plied the waters of North Carolina, most people will be quick to mention Edward Teach, the notorious Blackbeard, and a few would know Stede Bonnet and Captain Kidd. But after those, who would know of any others? Were there even other pirates of any note during the Golden Age?

Well, North Carolina was still in its infancy in the early 1700s. Only the towns of Bath, Edenton, and Beaufort were formed in the beginnings of the 18th century, from smaller, earlier settlements that were simple seaports or supply locations. Wilmington did not even exist until 1740, with the small settlement of nearby Brunswick Town not founded until 1726, both long after the last of the great pirates had fallen to the sword or hangman's noose. Even quaint little Ocracoke Village was not founded until 1715, and was mostly a settlement of pilots who operated small craft for the shallow waters of the sounds. There were no major deep water ports, and thus no ships and trade for pirates to pilfer.

What North Carolina did have was shelter and a wonderful quiet desolation. No one could see the pirates as they operated off of the coast. The many bays and inlets were great places to hide. Pirates could sneak out to pounce, then take their ill-gotten booty back up the rivers and bays in relative assurance that no one would see them, and none would be the wiser.

So while there may not be all the colorful places to go spend their treasure, or meet with like minded sailors like in the Caribbean, North Carolina did have its share of minor pirates that also either operated or met their end on its natural barrier island coast.

John Cole was a pirate that was captured off of the Hatteras coast. He sailed with Richard Worley and William Moody, other pirates that plied along the Carolina shores. He commanded a large ship named the *Eagle*, which he renamed *New York Revenge's Revenge*. The odd choice of names was because the ship was a tender for Richard Worley's ship, *New York Revenge*.

Cole was a short term pirate operating with the other sailors when he was pursued by a fleet put forth by South Carolina governor Robert Johnson. Governor Johnson had recently been successful in capturing Stede Bonnet, but was worried that there might be retribution by other pirates, especially with the planned hanging of the Gentleman Pirate. Johnson sent out a fleet to hunt down other pirates that might resume a blockade of Charles Town or take ships as they made their way in and out of the harbor. His fleet was able to find Richard Worley's ship first, since it was sailing at the harbor of Charles Town, but Worley was killed in the bloody battle. He and his crew had all sworn to fight to the death, and they kept their word.

Cole had split up with Worley, hoping to sail north and escape pursuit of Johnson's fleet, which included the captured *Revenge* of Stede Bonnet, along with ships that had been used to capture Bonnet the month before, in September of 1718. Thinking he would outrun the South Carolina ships, he sailed north with the plans of making to to Virginia, or perhaps the Chesapeake Bay. He should have turned into the sounds of North Carolina to hide, because only two hours after he was first spotted Johnson's fleet chased Cole down off of Cape Hatteras. He was quickly captured and taken back to Charles Town, where he met the same fate as any pirate, hanging at the end of a noose just off of Charles Town and buried in an unmarked grave in the marsh.

These pirates did not leave much of a mark on history, especially off the Carolina coast. No one sells figures of Moody or Cole at local gift shops. They did have some small measure of significance, not much, just a little, but something worth noticing even if their careers weren't really noticeable.

When Cole was captured, it ended a rather short career of piracy. The victorious naval militia made a discovery when they looked over Cole's ship for his captured treasure. It turned out that he had no gold, silver, or jewels. His hold was filled with prisoners, mostly women, who were shipped over from England in the *Eagle* before it had been taken by pirates. The women were originally sent to be sold into indentured servitude, essentially slaves, for the colonies. Even after their liberation from Cole, the fleet took them from the North Carolina coast to Charles Town, and then attempted to send them on to the Bahamas to force them into marriage to men there. Unfortunately the prisoners had not been cared for and all of them died of lack of food and water.

Richard Worley, a fairly successful pirate, has also been somewhat forgotten by history. But he did leave one mark that everyone who knows pirates would recognize. He had sailed from New York, across the Carolinas, and into the Spanish Main around the Bahamas. While he was in the Caribbean, he and his crew formed official articles, defining their jobs and how they split their prizes. One of the acts included creating their official colors. Their flag included a death's head along with crossed femur bones, which we now know as the infamous pirate flag the Jolly Roger. He may not have been the first or only pirate to fly the colors; many pirates had a similar flag. He just was the most successful pirate during the time to fly the Jolly Roger across the Carolina coasts.

Theodosia Burr

The only thing better than pirate stories are pirate ghost stories. Here's a spooky tale that takes place on Bald Head Island long ago.

Theodosia Burr never saw herself as a victim. She probably would have had good reason to feel that way. Her father became famous for being a killer. Aaron Burr was Vice President of the United States, serving with his own antagonist Thomas Jefferson, when Burr joined in a duel with Alexander Hamilton, killing him while Hamilton merely planned to fire in the air. Burr then may have tried to form his own country in the Louisiana Purchase and into Texas and Mexico, which led to Jefferson ordering his arrest for treason. Though Burr was acquitted, his reputation was ruined. Burr chose to go into exile rather than face the wrath of a nation that hated him.

His daughter Theodosia married a South Carolina wealthy planter Joseph Alston. He would go on to become not only a South Carolina representative, but governor of the state. Theodosia would suffer from frailty in health after the birth of her only son. Tragedy would later come in yet another wave, when their child would die at ten years old from malaria.

She would not even be able to travel to New York in July of 1812 to finally see her beloved father as he returned from exile. Her health did not permit her to travel. She may have known by that time that at only 29 years old, she had little time left to live. She possibly suffered from uterine cancer which is what made her so frail.

When she finally was able to travel in December of 1812 to see her father, Joseph Alston was unable to even travel with her, as he was needed to serve during the War of 1812.

So, on December 31, 1812, she was put aboard the good ship *Patriot*, a fast and tight schooner piloted by a skilled and trustworthy pilot. Her husband did his best to implore the captain to do everything to see his wife safely to New York.

So with all that had been handed to her, it would not be surprising if Theodosia saw herself as somewhat of a victim to a cruel, ruthless, and unforgiving fate.

Her next few days would prove that fate was not done with her, but she was not going to let fate make her a victim.

Somewhere off the coast of North Carolina, the good ship *Patriot*, with Theodosia Burr-Alston aboard, would disappear with all hands, never to be seen again. No one knows what happened to Theodosia or anyone else. There are several rumors and suspicions, including her falling to the notorious Breakers of the Outer Banks, but there is another story, too.

And it of course involves pirates.

Now, by 1813, pirates would seem to have been a thing of the long past. It would have been almost one hundred years since Blackbeard and his notorious cohorts felt the end of a sword or a noose. Pirates were no more by the time that the *Patriot* sailed up the North Carolina coast, weren't they?

The early 1800s were actually a new heyday for pirates, and one in which they were much more ruthless, bloodthirsty, heartless, and indescribably violent. Spanish pirates based in Cuba were sailing across the Caribbean and up the Florida coast, taking ships and leaving none to tell the tale. It is suspected that Spanish pirates, lying in wait at Smiths Island, known today as Bald Head Island, were able to sail out and take the *Patriot* and all aboard as it passed the shallow banks just offshore.

The legend tells a rather strange and unbelievable story. It may have been the young and ruthless Roberto Cofrecinas, or another of the many violent pirates that plied Atlantic waters that captured the ship. All aboard were quickly and horribly dispatched. But the captain knew that in Theodosia he had someone of greater value alive than dead. She was young and beautiful, certainly, and could fetch a price for that alone. But she might be worth even more if she was ransomed off. Her husband and her father would pay well to have her back.

He placed her ashore, under the guard of two crew members, while he decided what he would do with the young Theodosia.

At the time, Smiths Island was still empty, undeveloped. Old Baldy, the iconic lighthouse, the oldest in the state, had not even been built yet. The original light that stood on the southwest of the island had long been destroyed, so there were no structures on the island, nor were there any people, besides poor Theodosia and her two captors.

The pirates decided to make the best of their easy assignment, and proceeded to get incredibly drunk on rum until they passed out.

At that moment, Theodosia took her chance to escape. She freed herself from her bonds and ran off into the island. It took her little time to discover it *was* only an island. There was nowhere for her to go, no shelter to hide her, and she had no skills to survive off of the land, especially in her poor health.

Her predicament was made worse when the pirates woke up. The fact that it was their captain, both sober and furious, that woke them up made it much, much worse. He was infuriated that the pirates had lost his prize, and threatened them with a most exquisite death if they didn't acquire Theodosia.

The two pirates began their search in earnest.

Theodosia not only realized that she was on an island, but that the island was small. Smiths Island was actually made up of smaller islands, disconnected by low waters and impassable marshes. Bald Head Island was just that, a smooth, sandy bald hill of sand, with little in the way of hiding even in the rolling dunes and sea grasses. The two pirates, well inspired, quickly tracked down Theodosia, and the chase was on.

Theodosia, wearing a beautiful white dress, and both hungry and sick, knew the two pirates would soon capture her, and then do unspeakable things to her. She had seen how they had treated her captain and crew. With her time on earth now shortened to hours, Theodosia made a decision.

She had never seen herself as a victim.

As the pirates closed in on her, Theodosia had nowhere else to go. She would be chased down, caught, tortured, and killed. She knew her fate.

So she chose not to be their victim. Theodosia picked up her dress and walked into the cold January waves of the churning Atlantic Ocean. The dress that she wore, once so beautiful, was quickly soaked through with salt water. She wasn't strong enough to keep her balance, and she didn't care.

The waves knocked her down, and the current pulled her under. She was swept out into the depths, the prize so desired by the pirates now lost to the sea.

Incensed by his loss, Captain Cofrecinas lashed out in anger. He pulled his cutlass and in a fit of rage cut the heads off of the two pirates tasked with guarding Theodosia. He then left their bodies on the beach to be picked clean by the scuttling ghost crabs, who would feast without judgement on the pirates' bodies. They would receive no burial, no marker, not even the decency of being swept away by the waves.

So the death of three people on the shore of Bald Head Island is the end of a sad, tragic story that may or may not have even happened. No one really knows. Spanish pirates did operate off the shores on rare occasion, and Theodosia Burr-Alston was lost somewhere off the coast of North Carolina, but there were no documents or confessions to look to.

But there is a little bit of rather strange evidence that it just might be true.

To this day, residents and guests to Bald Head Island have told stories of seeing a ghostly vision in white. A young woman walks the land, a wistful figure of gossamer and cloud only. Not fully formed, she has been seen on the beach, the trails, and by the light. The ghost of Theodosia Burr-Alston is thought to still walk the land of her last days. She hopes to one day somehow find a way off the island, onto a ship, and on her way to New York to finally meet with her father.

Many people have spied the ghost of Theodosia. One of the most interesting parts of the legend is that the first thing one notices is not her ethereal figure, but that she has a distinct sweet aroma. First you notice her perfume before she appears, and as she dissipates into the ether, the last thing that is left is the faint wisps of flowers.

And the pirates? Well, it is a more obscure tale, no longer told, but the pirates were once seen on the island, too. They were known to chase down people who would slip off to the island for clandestine meetings on the darkened and empty beaches. It was noticed back in the 1930s that the few times it was reported that the strange headless Spanish pirate ghosts were encountered on Bald Head, they only seemed to pursue young ladies with short, dark hair.

Only those that looked suspiciously like Theodosia.

The Cora Tree

Sometimes it doesn't take a pirate to do something bad. Sometimes it is just a villain showing up that causes all the problems.
Or is it?

Sometime in the early 1700s, right before the height of the Golden Age of Piracy, a young woman and her baby appeared in a small village on Hatteras Island. The land that would much later become the village of Frisco had several families living in the soundside forest. The houses there were meager buildings, simply constructed to provide shelter from the winds, sun, and storms that raked across Hatteras Island in unpredictable waves. The people there were mostly shipwreck victims themselves, who came from farther north in search of decent game, land, and fish to survive and make some form of life on the rugged coast. They built their houses on the west side, away from the stinging salt winds and pounding waves that were already quickly becoming the Graveyard of the Atlantic.

They may not know how a strange woman and her babe in arms appeared on their island, but they could understand why she was there. In years past, far up north, women had been persecuted after being accused of being witches, and an isolated island far to the south was a good place to hide from the modern, enlightened world that treated a young unmarried woman with a baby as a pariah. The locals, with quiet respect, paid her no mind as she set up a cabin on the sound not too close to the village, where she and her little knee-baby could live in solitude as she caught fish and crabs in nets in the sound.

They knew little about her, except for her name, Cora.

And that she was likely a witch.

Curiosity often got the better of some villagers. They wondered just how her crops grew so well, and how her nets were full. Her baby never cried, but neither did he laugh or giggle. The child, almost always in her arms, had a serious, stoic stare, as if to warn off any person when they got too close. One time a boy of the village, as aggressive boys might do, made a mean face at the strange child. Rather than scold the boy, Cora did nothing. But the next night, the boy came down with a horrendous fever, and remained sick for several days and nights, teetering upon death as he burned from his illness.

A local fisherman, Thomas Smith, a leader of the town, did what little he could. He placed a bushel of his own catch, along with some prize vegetables, a rare fruit, and some onions, on her dock. The very day, the boy's fever broke.

Another time as she walked down one of the dusty sand roads of the little villages, a local pushed his cow across the path, into Cora. The rude behavior was not addressed, but

Cora did run one long finger across the cow's side. When he got his cow home, the villager discovered that his prized cow would no longer give milk.

So, with little doubt, the villagers of Hatteras knew that Cora was a witch, and gave her a wide berth.

And that was the way it was for them. Peace was found in the balance.

But one summer, the balance would be horribly thrown off with the arrival of a stranger and his strange entourage. Captain Eli Blood, skipper of the brig *Susan G.* and his crew of miscreants, rough sailors, and freed Barbadan slaves washed ashore when their ship became waterlogged and in danger of sinking. In order to save his ship and the precious cargo, he was able to careen the ship and unload his supplies. Word would be sent to his masters far up in New England to send for another ship and supplies to make repairs. Until then, Captain Blood and his wild crew were the guests of the people of Hatteras.

His sailors would spend their days and nights on the beach. They set the sails up to shelter them from the sun and wind, and used the crates of their cargo to build a makeshift town on the shore. They then proceeded to enjoy life in wild abandon, with no duties to perform. Life was good for them, even if it was a little wild. They liked the wild life.

Captain Blood, being a captain, was due a little more respect. Captain Smith put up the New England firebrand of a captain in his own modest home. And by put up, Smith also put up with Captain Blood's rather rough and loud proclamations and tales. But it was his duty as a fellow sailor to offer aid in times of distress, even on land. And Captain Blood was at least hospitable. He accepted the meager offerings with no complaints.

Captain Blood would tell stories of his life in the cold and more developed New England, where the roads were straight and the buildings tight. He also assailed anyone who would listen to the stories of witches in the woods, and how they had rounded up several girls and gotten them to admit their guilt and change their ways. It all seemed horribly invasive to the poor locals, who were very used to minding their own business.

But it did lead to Captain Blood discovering that there very well might be a witch in their very midst, right here on Hatteras. He was nearly insufferable when he learned of Cora. It was all the locals could do to get him to promise to leave her be. They needed no more problems with the solitary woman and her child.

Captain Blood kept his word to leave her alone.

Right up until a young man was found dead on the beach by his crew.

He was a young, handsome boy at one time. He was known in the village, living in a nearby settlement. He seemed like a popular young man, handsome, well liked, and with no one wanting to harm him. But when he was found, his face was waterlogged from being in the ocean, and his visage was a rictus of terror. He had surely seen something that had frightened him to death. There was no marking of any kind on his body to show how he died, except strange scratches on his forehead. When the crew looked at the wounds, they swore they saw the marks of a demon on him.

Captain Blood was brought out and shown the poor boy. He immediately noticed both the scratches on the young man's head, as well as tiny footprints leading away from the body, into the woods. Being from New England, he saw himself as an expert on witches, and proclaimed that this must be the work of Cora the Witch. He and his crew formed a mob to go into the forest by the sound to capture Cora, and if need be, mete out a deserved punishment.

As they stormed through the little village, many people pleaded with them to think before acting. The locals felt bad for the loss of the boy, but he may have just died in the ocean, having fallen overboard and drowned. It sadly happened more often than they would have liked. Life was sometimes short and tragic on Hatteras. They understood that, even if they didn't like to accept it.

But Captain Blood and his crew, warmed on revenge and fortified with courage from a rum bottle, heard none of it. He went to Cora's hut on the sound, broke the door down, and dragged the poor young woman out.

Again, Captain Smith pleaded with Blood. He insisted that she be given a fair chance, that she be taken before a magistrate inland, to hear her case. Blood decided he was judge enough, that he would test her to be a witch.

First, as both his crew and the poor villagers watched, cowed by the violent captain and drunken mad crew, Captain Blood took the bound Cora and threw her into the sound. He stated that this was his first test. Any witch would use her dark magic to save herself and float, while a mere mortal would simply drown.

In the shallow water, Cora struggled and was somehow able to remain upright, as she gasped for air. Blood decried that she passed the first test.

Then, grabbing her by the hair and dragging her to shore, he pulled his ship's knife. It was dull and jagged, roughed by cutting and splitting rope, but with a sharp point at the end. He took the knife and placed it into her wet hair and tried to cut it. The thick bundle was pulled tight, and he was not able to cut through her long locks. He declared it to be like wire, uncuttable. She had passed the second test.

He then took the point of his knife and cut into her hand, dripping her blood into an old pail. He poked his own finger and let the drops of blood intermingle with the brackish sound water. There, he and his crew stared to divine her true intentions. All of those that looked swore they saw Cora cavorting with the devil himself.

Now sure she was a witch, the crew took her and her little baby, for they were sure that this child was supernatural, most likely a shapeshifting familiar, like a witch's black cat, and then carried them both to a large tree in an open spot in the woods near the village. She was bound with rope wrapped around the tree, her baby still in her arms, uncrying, glaring in hate and anger. The crew set out gathering tinder to be placed around her. They planned on disposing of the witch the way they knew how. They were going to burn Cora at the tree.

Again, one last time, Captain Smith pleaded with Blood not to do this. Cora may have been guilty, but it would be up to a judge to decide, not some makeshift court.

Blood heard none of the words. He merely pushed Smith aside as he began to approach the kindling with his lit torch.

As he walked forward, the sky grew darker and darker. Once a beautiful day of blue skies, now the air was ominous, filled with blackening clouds. With every step that Blood made, the weather worsened. Far off, rain began to pelt down in sheets. Thunder rolled and lightning split the black skies.

Most of the village ran in terror from the approaching supernatural storm. Even the crew began to step back, sobering with the change in the temperature.

But Captain Blood was made of stronger stuff. No witchcraft would stop him, he swore. He approached with the torch as rain began to fall, making hissing noises as heavy drops found the fire he held. Then, as he lowered the torch to the wood...

There was a tremendous explosion!

Lightning crackled with anger and intent right onto the big tree. The blast knocked back all that stood by. Captain Blood, the closest, was thrown back from the tree, knocked unconscious by the mighty strike. His boots fell from him, and his jacket smoked.

When they all awoke, Captain Blood the last to revive, they discovered something amazing. The tree had been split down the middle to the trunk. It smoldered with fire, and the scent of brimstone hung heavy in the air, choking the few people left. At the tree, the ropes were still bound tight, without an inch of give to them.

But Cora and her babe were gone. Vanished into the cloudy ether. The storm dissipated as quickly as it formed, with blue skies appearing as white clouds quickly parted.

Still unsure as to what had happened, Captains Blood and Smith walked toward the tree. There was no Cora, but the wood at her feet had not been consumed in a fire. It had not even been scorched or singed. But there was one sign that they saw all too well.

There, on the tree, as if etched into the bark at the trunk with a fiery finger were four letters, spelling out her name.

CORA

Terrified and aggrieved, Blood was ashamed at having lost his trophy. He was shunned from the village, and had to await rescue at the beach with no help or support from the Hatteras villagers. They made no attempt to see him, and only counted the days until he and his crew could be removed from the island.

Cora never appeared again. The village was in equal fear that one day she and her child would come back and seek out revenge against the people. Captain Smith kept a wary eye out at her shack, in case he ever saw movement there. He would go by, looking in, but discovered it to be empty, devoid of all signs of habitation, as if Cora had never been there at all.

A few of the villagers would speak in quiet tones, always inside, away from prying ears, in case they were ever overheard. They discussed the evil that Captain Blood brought. His crew had been wild, violent, untrustworthy, and dangerous. The captain was uncontrollable, unwilling to follow the rules of law and of the society he was thrust upon.

But then, as quiet as they could, some would say,...

"But she was still a witch."

Operation Drumbeat

What makes a pirate? Is it the sneaky treachery of a deceptive attack on an unarmed ship? Or the cocky charms of the rogues while on land? And could there be something even worse?

Piracy on the high seas has become a glamorous history in these modern times. There's just something about a swashbuckling rogue riding the high seas, bedecked in a long flowing black cloat, a weather eye out for merchant ships overloaded and fat with treasure that would normally be taken to wealthy barons to extend their prosperity and luxury, at the long suffering hands of hard laboring crews. A pirate, in modern view, has almost become a Robin Hood figure, a hero that took from the rich and gave, with a little bit in his own pocket, to the poor.

But what really defines a pirate? We only picture them from the Golden Age, that era of the tall ships, sailing from the Caribbean to New York, or Spanish galleons loaded with ill-gotten cursed gold, all ready for the taking. Long black hair, a rugged scar from a lesson learned early, the pirates we see in our daydreams are just that, dreamy figures of a certain time.

But when we expand our view, the pirates become more ruthless, less colorful, more villain than rogue.

Pirates judged by their actions are much worse than pirates defined by their clothes. And when we look at a different time, a different definition, we see some pirates as who they really are. Horrid, callous, sneaky creatures, dirty, hiding in the night, taking lives without recompense or concern.

That's just what the Outer Banks saw for six months of 1942, when its coast was the home of a new breed of pirate, the Nazi U-boat.

World War II had been raging in Europe for two years and in Asia even years longer when Japan attacked Pearl Harbor in far off Hawaii. While it couldn't have been farther away for the residents of the Outer Banks, the attack hit home with them in more than one way. Several locals had family in the U.S. Navy and they were worried that they may have lost someone in the attack.

In a much grander sense, the attack in Hawaii meant that now the U.S. was at war, not only with Japan, but with the rest of the Axis powers in Europe, including Germany. And that would bring the war much, much closer to North Carolina than they were prepared for.

Before December 7th, 1941, the U.S. played their neutrality to the hilt, which allowed them to run supplies to war strapped Great Britain, without which the island fortress would fold under the relentless pressure of fighting the German war machine. The German Kriegsmarine could not attack the U.S. ships without waking the burgeoning military of America. But with the attack on Hawaii and the resulting declaration of war by Nazi Germany, the gloves were off.

Karl Dönitz was supreme commander of the U-boats of the Nazi Kriegsmarine, their navy. He saw a potential weakness in the steady supply of material, and especially oil, that was moving from the U.S. Atlantic coast to Great Britain. If the Nazis could slow that shipping down, it could dry up the fuel of war. Dönitz, and his staff officer Gunther Hessler, who was also his son-in-law, calculated that if they could send 800,000 tons of shipping to the bottom of the Atlantic every month, Great Britain would be sent back to the stone age. To do this, Dönitz had a secret weapon, and a slightly less secret weapon.

The less secret weapon was his fleet of U-boats. His secret weapon was Victor Oehrn. Oehrn was a member of Dönitz's staff, and a skilled military planner. It was Oehrn who did most of the attack designs for the U-boat fleet. Dönitz just got all the credit.

What Oehrn saw when he looked at a map of the U.S. east coast were two distinct coastlines. One was the active and busy ports of the north, full of ships as well as bases for the U.S. military might. But the other was a coastline devoid of not only military bases, but also almost empty of people. There was one place that not only had nothing in the way of naval patrols, but also pushed shipping close to the coast, while still dropping the ocean depths off a cliff just offshore. It was Cape Hatteras, North Carolina.

Dönitz would take the plans and ideas that Oehrn had and run up the very short chain of command he had. Dönitz wanted to send at least twelve of his U-boats to the American shores, packed with fuel and loaded with torpedoes, shells, and bullets, with the idea that they would lay in wait at the quiet, pristine hunting grounds across the eastern seaboard, resting on the sandy bottom during the days, and then rise up at night to take the unsuspecting ships unaware until the first explosions sent sailors into a cold January sea. He even hoped that the attacks could be timed out to the hour, on the same night.

The plan was named Operation Paukenschlag. Drumbeat.

Dönitz wanted his twelve U-boats, but got only six for the initial operation. One would turn back with mechanical problems, leaving only five, but those boats would leave a very dirty scalding mark on the North Carolina coast.

These were wartime belligerents, not pirates in the classic sense, certainly. But in many ways they were like pirates. In Laurient, on the coast of occupied France where the U-boats were based, the submariners in their all black uniforms walked around like they thought they were movie stars. Cocky, self-assured, with no one willing to cross their path for fear of reprisal, they were an easily recognizable part of the port city.

But when they made their way to the Atlantic coast and North Carolina, no one saw them as they were, dirty, oil covered, foul smelling from being trapped for days in stale air underwater. And no one saw them still when at night they arose to deal death to an unsuspecting nation.

The people of the Outer Banks would have a front row seat to the carnage.

On January 18, 1942, U-boats began setting up their firing range on the Cape Hatteras coast. Captain Richard Zapp of *U-66* and Reinhard Hardegen of *U-123* had arrived. Hardegen had already tasted success with four ships sunk around New York, but felt that hunting would be easier and safer at Cape Hatteras now that the U.S. was alerted to his presence farther north. He would quickly discover how good his targets would be on that first night off Cape Hatteras as his watch officers alerted him to a fireball at sea. Zapp had struck first, He torpedoed the oil tanker *Allan Jackson*, splitting it in half, spilling its fiery contents into the sea, along with its crew. Most of the sailors on the *Jackson* would die by drowning or being drawn into the oily blaze on the surface. Zapp would not surface to see if he could give aid to the survivors, nor did he care to learn the name of the ship he sank.

Within a day, the two U-boats would chase down and sink three more ships. One would prove to be a most horrific and colorful attack, that would make it known to everyone on the Outer Banks that the U-boats were on the prowl.

At 2 a.m. local time, the ship bell for the *City of Atlanta* rang four times, marking the middle watch. They were just passing Bodie Island Lighthouse only a few miles to the west, with Cape Hatteras dead ahead. Most of the crew of 47 were asleep or off duty, and Captain Leman Urquhart probably couldn't sleep. He would have already heard the sinking of the *Jackson* far off to sea, so far that he would not see it. He kept his ship close to shore, in the shallows, where he hoped no U-boat would operate. He also ran without most lights, though he still kept his green and red sidelights on, as well as a bow light. The cold waters of the coast could be empty, but could also get crowded with ships as they traveled from north to south, and back again. A risk of attack from a U-boat seemed only equally risky to a collision with another ship.

At the time, the U.S. was woefully unprepared for the war to come to home. The lights of Avon, just to the east, still burned brightly late into the night, which allowed for even blacked out ships to be easily seen in silhouette as they passed by.

But the *U-123* and Captain Hardegan sat just further offshore, surfaced, but in the darkness to the west and unseen by anyone not already onboard the submarine. Hardegan sighted the *Atlanta* easily, using the mechanical computers from his tower mounted binoculars to plot a clear course for his torpedoes. He watched the *Atlanta* for a while. It was a smaller freighter, heading south to its home in Savannah, and probably carried nothing of military value if was going that direction. Still, to Hardegan, it was tonnage, and the numbers were all that mattered. He needed to unload his torpedoes on something, and this target just swam up to him.

He calculated the timing of the torpedo run, and with the simple command in German, *"Los,"* the huge G7 torpedo began its run. It would only take fifteen seconds, they were so close. There wouldn't have been enough time for a warning even if the torpedo had been spotted by the few members of the crew on deck.

The torpedo struck directly into the engine room. The blast was so strong and so close that shrapnel rained down upon the sailors of the *U-123*. But for the crew on the *Atlanta*, it was so much worse.

The engine room crew were killed instantly in the blast, which might have been fortunate. The coaling bunker filled with cold salt water, drowning the coal passers in the icy water.

Most of the crew would not even escape the ship as it filled then sank in shallow water. Many of the life boats were not even able to be deployed while the ship listed to port. Half the lifeboats could not reach the water, while the starboard ones were broken and crashing uncontrollably into the ocean. Most of the surviving crew were washed overboard. At the time, the *Atlanta* was so close to shore that it had found the converse south traveling Labrador Current, an icy river that filled in when the warmer Gulf Stream pushed out into the Atlantic Ocean. The water was a horribly cold 47 degrees in January. Most of the crew would die of hypothermia, their dead bodies bobbing in lifejackets that did nothing to save their lives from the bitter cold.

Only four people of the 47 would survive the night. George Tavelle, Robert Fennell, Earl Dowdy, and a nearly frozen John York would be picked up at 8 a.m. by the passing *SS Seatrain Texas*. Captain Albert Dalzell took a considerable risk by lowering a rescue boat for the four men. He and everyone now knew there was a U-boat in the area, and any ship stopping would be an easy target. The ship made way even as the little rescue boat was being hoisted back aboard.

Sadly, John York would die of hypothermia as soon as he was brought on board.

As tragic and horrid as the attack was, it did one other thing. The explosion was so close to shore, that even in the night, it awoke the residents across Hatteras Island. Residents of the three little villages of Rodanthe, Waves, and Salvo, along with farther south at Avon and Buxton, woke to their windows rattling from the explosion just offshore. They would look out their windows early in the dark morning to see a huge orange fireball just offshore. They wouldn't know the name of the ship. They really wouldn't know anything of what was going on. But they *knew*.

War had come to Hatteras, which meant war had come to America.

More ships would sink over the next several months, and the Nazi drumbeat would get louder and louder for the locals. Kids used to going to the beach would soon find washed up pieces of the ships sunk in attacks, along with the requisite bodies, bloated or burned, hardly anything like the more jovial pastime of collecting pretty shells along the shoreline.

Those bodies had to be collected, identified, and if possible, stored and shipped to loved ones for a proper burial. When that wasn't possible, some of the bodies had to be interred almost where they were found, like the victims of shipwrecks long ago.

Identifying bodies was a rather horrific task, but one that had to be done. The job fell to Aycock Brown to find out who these poor lost souls were. And that job was a part of the story of two of the more tragic sinkings.

The *San Delfino* was an eight thousand ton oil tanker carrying aviation gas and ammunition when it passed off of the Hatteras coast late on April 9, 1942. *U-203* commander Rolf Mutzelburg spied the ship even as the *San Delfino* ran blacked out and zigzagging at its highest speed. He placed a torpedo in the ship, but the sturdy *San Delfino* tried to outrun the hidden U-boat. Mutzelburg fired two more torpedoes, but missed with both. His dander up, the U-boat commander had to chase down the fast but wounded tanker and finally plot for his third attack. This torpedo would find its mark, cracking the ship open, spilling out the lighter aviation fuel onto the water and igniting the ammunition in a huge explosion. The ship burned with a hellish light. Captain Albert Gumbleton knew his ship was lost, and gave the order to abandon ship.

When the first lifeboat was put over with 28 crew aboard, they were immediately sucked into the sinking ship and the burning fuel. All crew would tragically die in flames while surrounded by a cruel and unforgiving cold ocean that could do nothing to extinguish the fire.

The men in a second lifeboat saw the tragedy and with superhuman effort pulled themselves away from the flames to be rescued by a fishing trawler.

When one of the bodies washed ashore, Aycock Brown was sent in to see who it was. He knew it was one of three possibilities, a merchant seaman, an Allied sailor, or an enemy, but whoever it was, he was certainly dead. Brown discovered through fingerprints that the man was Michael Cairns, an officer from the *San Delfino*.

Realizing the body was a British officer, far from his island home and loved ones, Brown wanted to at least honor the man in death. He had no honor guard, and no sailors even to stand in mourning. So Brown flew to Morehead City to find a British ship at berth in the hopes that some men could come to the sailor's burial at a small plot in the shadow of the Cape Hatteras lighthouse.

He found the British submarine patrol ship *Bedforshire*, a trawler converted to anti-submarine warfare and loaned to the U.S. in hopes of stemming the tide of attacks. It was commanded by a handsome and affable commander, sub-lieutenant Thomas Cunningham. Brown asked if he could have a few British flags or naval ensigns to shroud the coffin of Cairns, along with some sailors to stand in honor of the fallen man. Cunningham immediately invited Brown to his wardroom for a drink, a tradition in the British navy of having a sip of rum once a day. The sip turned into a bottle, and the two parted, not quite sober, but certainly friends.

Cunningham would not be able to spare any men, for he had to put out as soon as refueling was done the next morning, but he could spare four Union Jacks. Cunningham, while a happy man who was celebrating the upcoming birth of his first son, deftly included two more than requested, as he knew that Brown would likely need them in the future.

It was a sadly prescient act by the commander.

It would be about six weeks later when Brown would again be called upon to identify the recovered bodies of a sinking, this time arriving at Ocracoke Island. He normally would use a simple fingerprint kit, take imprints, and match them with known prints of sailors, if there were no other identifying marks or papers. In this case, as the sheet was pulled from the bodies stored in an impromptu morgue at the life-saving station in Ocracoke village, Brown needed none of his tools to identify the body of his friend Thomas Cunningham.

While Brown was sure that the *Bedfordshire* had been sunk, there had been no radio call, and no sign of debris. It wouldn't be until after the war that the Allies were able to determine that the *Bedfordshire* had been sunk by a single torpedo from *U-558*, the only submarine in the area at the time.

Brown had seethed at the death of his friend, knowing there would be a child growing up without a father somewhere on the other side of the Atlantic. Cunningham might be one of many to lose their lives at the Nazi drumbeat, but Brown had known him, drank with him, and liked him. While Brown could do nothing to get his hands on the Nazis that had killed his new friend, he did organize as best he could an honor guard for the fallen sailors. One of the two spare British flags that Cunningham had given Brown was used on his coffin. Only Cunningham and Telegraph Operator Stanley Craig were identified. Two other sailors, their names unknown but likely from the *Bedfordshire*, were also buried in a small plot of Ocracoke, donated by the Williams family, just outside their brick walled family cemetery.

Thomas Cunningham's widow, Barbara, had asked if the Catholic Rites of Burial had been performed at his grave. With no time and no access to a priest, Brown and the local sailors had only done the best they could. By the end of 1942, a Catholic chaplain was able to provide the last rites for Cunningham, along with a Protestant pastor to speak for the unidentified dead.

That began a tradition of care for the cemetery by local sailors who felt a kinship with the fallen British mariners. Over the decades, the local coast guard proffered care for the cemetery, with an annual somber celebration of the loss of the four men and their never found crew members. All thirty seven sailors on the *Bedfordshire* were lost, with thirty three lost at sea after the attack.

The loss of the *San Delfino* and the *Bedfordshire* are only visible markers of a much greater threat from the U-boats across the Carolina coast. The graves of their crews stand in quiet tribute to their lives, while the bulk of the men and women that sailed across the coast would never be found.

Nazi U-boats targeted ships with no thought to military value. Passengers and crew were of equal value to the German torpedoes, and the value was nil. Only tonnage mattered to the Nazis, not lives.

The U.S. would fail to respond quickly to the threat, with few military ships committed to patrolling the coast. They would first try with the U.S. Navy Armed Guard, where merchant ships were armed with deck guns in the vain hope of hitting a hidden U-boat in the dark during an attack on a pitching ship. The Armed Guard ended up having losses higher in percentage than any other arm of the U.S. military.

The U.S. finally got a small measure of payback from one of its old destroyers from the end of the last great war, the *USS Jesse Roper*. The *Roper* was an old destroyer built in 1918, and had not fired a shot in anger since. The Captain, Lieutenant Commander Hamilton Howe, had been close friends with the captain of the *Jacob Jones*, a sister ship to the *Roper*, which had been sunk by a U-boat torpedo. He wanted payback, as did all the crew. When they found a submarine, the *U-85*, in the darkness with their new secret weapon, a radar array recently placed onboard the *Roper*, Howe was ready to chase the submarine down.

It would be a strange game of chase, as the U-boat and destroyer circled each other from hundreds of yards away, each trying to get into a firing position. The *U-85* had loosed a torpedo at the following *Roper*, cutting a luminescent line through the ocean and the stirred plankton that glowed with the agitation of the torpedo's wake, but had missed.

Now it was the *Roper*'s turn.

The order was given for the crew, over a hundred men arming ten deck guns, to open fire as a spotlight lit up the U-boat, only seven hundred yards away. Unfortunately, even as the crew had been practiced and skilled in the operation of the guns, all of them failed, one after the other, from jams caused by the salt spray and nonfunctioning ammunition. As they struggled at their weapons, the U-boat crew readied their 88mm deck gun. It could easily put a deadly hole in the *Roper* with one well placed shot.

Chief Bosun's mate Jack Wright cleared a jam in a machine gun, with the colorful cursing only a Navy man could know, and began to open fire on the downrange Kriegsmarine sailors. The bullets tore through the Nazi sailors, stopping them from operating their own big gun. But it wouldn't sink a U-boat.

But a big .50 caliber deck gun would.

Harry Heyman manned the stern gun, and saw everything that was happening as his ship slowly turned to give him both range and access to his target. His gun was already loaded. He simply aimed at the U-boat and ordered "Fire!"

The projectile, an armor piercing round that would poke a hole through the U-boat like God's hammer pounding a nail, would travel at well over 2,000 feet per second. At only seven hundred yards, it would cover the ground in fractions of a second, though the shot would be visible by all as it traversed the distance. While the *Roper* would shudder from the shot, the U-85 would be mortally wounded.

The U-boat almost immediately began to fill with water from a hole just below the waterline amidships. While some of the sailors would find their way into a cold ocean, many would not escape the waterfall of salt water that poured into the stern half of the U-boat.

Seeing the U-boat sinking gave both hope and fear to the captain and officers of the *Roper*. They were unsure as to whether the *U-85* was sunk or merely diving in order to deliver another torpedo attack. Captain Howe would order his ship to circle the area with depth charges. By the time he had arrived at the place where the U-boat had been, his sonar operator had picked up a strong signal of something under the water. He had to be sure that his ship and crew didn't join the Nazis already in the water. He knew he was signing a death sentence for the Germans that had jumped off the U-boat. With every explosion, more men died, but he had to be sure to rid the ocean of this one threat.

So the Roper was able to get a measure of revenge on the submarine that sank the *Jacob Jones*, along with other merchant ships.

Before the summer, thousands more people, innocent merchants and passengers, would go down off the coast of North Carolina. Most would never know the attack was coming, dying in the darkness, or left abandoned on rafts to float away into the Atlantic, never to be seen or rescued.

The Nazi sinkings would leave their marks in other ways. The ships they sank would spill their oil and fuel, whether they carried it as cargo or just for power. The oil would wash up on beaches, clogging wildlife, polluting the fishing waters, and making what was once a beautiful pristine beach into a toxic netherworld, forbidden to be accessed by anyone on the shore.

The oil would remain. In the Seventies and Eighties, it was a required addition to every beach house to have a glass bottle of vegetable oil and a roll of paper towels on hand. Invariably, a stroll on the beach would lead to tar on the heels of everyone, local and visitor alike. Only a diligent scrub with an oil soaked towel would get rid of the black tar stuck to a kid's foot.

While pirates certainly made their mark on our coast, they have long since left us. The Golden Age of piracy ended with little left for the world to find. Far worse were the villains of the 1940s, the U-boats who may have raided commerce like the pirates of old, but with much worse damage. Death and destruction was literally in their wake, and the scars of their actions still are there, just beneath the surface. A pirate's treasure may hide under our sands, somewhere. But the Nazi rewards are much more a stain on the coast of North Carolina.

Otway Burns

Pirate or politician, which one is worse? One North Carolinian turned out to be both, and far from becoming hated or feared, he became a bit of a hero.

Privateers would prove to be of extreme importance the the newly formed United States. While the boat builders in the northern states could shape a fast and svelte craft, they always needed a crew, and a skilled one at that. At the time, many men looked to the sea for action, adventure, and a paycheck, but not all were one with the ways of the ocean and sail.

Otway Burns would be born for the task, however. He would become an amazing skipper, and then a hero to a nation. And it would all happen beginning in the little port town of Swansboro, NC. He grew up learning his trade by navigating the shallow sounds with unprecedented skill, which would show in later years when he became a seafaring captain. As an adult, he built ships in Beaufort, and practiced his trade in merchant ships from North Carolina all the way up to Maine.

When the War of 1812 came to the new nation, while there were ships, there was a need for sailors, and even more so captains with skill and will. A privateer with a fast ship would offer both reward for the man willing to go into commerce raiding, as well as offer a cost effective way for the nation to supplement its meager navy. So when Otway Burns discovered that war had been declared between the U.S. and Britain, he saw the opportunity. He just had to wait a moment to seize it.

After sailing from Portland, Maine with rejected offers for his little coast ship, he put in to New York and spied a lithe vessel, barely 70 feet long, but low, well armed. He purchased the ship *Levere* and had her masts refitted with yards to allow a quick sail replacement. She would prove to be hard to hit, and even harder to chase down. Burns renamed the ship the *Snap Dragon*, and legend was born.

The legend was born, but it still had to be crewed. Instead of signing on crew for pay, he headed to New Bern and took on shareholders. The crew would be privateers, taking from British merchants, and they would get a cut of what they took. It was a way of inspiring the crew to fight, as well as giving them value in the craft. It would prove to be incredibly profitable to almost all the men who served. As long as they survived.

Getting the crew actually posed Burns' first problem. The officials of New Bern took a dim view of privateers. They saw it as licensed thievery, and did what they could to finagle arrests of any man who signed on. Soon Burns would take his crew aboard the ship for protection. When a group of six process servers tried to row themselves out, Burns overturned their little boat, forcing them to cling to the keel as they kicked back to shore unceremoniously, and without their prizes.

When a lawyer began hurling epithets at Burns and the ship, Burns rowed ashore and threw the lawyer into the river. He even kicked the lawyer back in as he climbed onto the dock, refusing to let the man get out of the water until he apologized. Burns would realize he could not fulfill his crew in New Bern, and sailed to Norfolk to finish the work.

It would be the beginning of the first of three voyages that would end up being the most daring, adventurous, and dashing escapades of the war of 1812. Burns would go on to become both a multimillionaire and a hero to the nation.

His first trip would send him to the hot waters of the Caribbean, where he would take merchant ships as prizes, stock his hold full, and commit to a daring midnight trip into the harbor of the enemy.

Burns had become such a problem with merchant ships in the Caribbean that the British sent a warship out to hunt him down. The brig *Nettler* was a low slung ship with two tall masts, fast, well armed, powerful and dangerous to the little *Snap Dragon*. Unfortunately it was also undermanned for the number of guns it had. Early in the morning, a crew member of the *Snap Dragon* spotted tall sails on the horizon. Burns recognized the ship as the *Nettler* as soon as it was within spyglass distance. Burns declared he was tired of running from these warships, and turned to the approaching threat instead of sailing for the horizon. Burns knew the *Nettler* was short handed, and that he probably had the upper hand.

The commander of the *Nettler* saw the *Snap Dragon* turn toward him, and realized he was in a precarious position. He then turned and ran, with Burns in pursuit. The chase would last for twelve long hours, from early morning to the beginning of evening, when the *Nettler* finally thought it would find safety under the guns of the fort at Tortola.

Burns was having none of it. He hoisted the British colors and sailed past the fort before the crew of the *Nettler* could get ashore and get word that the *Snap Dragon* was closing. Burns passed safely by the fort and nestled itself into the port of Tortola under the cover of darkness.

Burns, feeling his success, then decided to take some of the merchant ships at anchor in the harbor. He sent crews on rowboats with their oarlocks wrapped in cloth to make them silent toward a darkened and still merchant vessel. They passed quietly across the water, under the only watchful eyes they saw, a flock of white sheep on a hill that slept in the starlight.

Unfortunately, they were spotted and hailed. When the hail was not answered correctly, the ship dropped pretenses and opened fire with its guns. The merchant ship turned out to be the *Nettler*, with its crew armed and prepared.

The crew of the *Snap Dragon* retreated under fire. Not only did the ship fire at them, but the sheep did, too. It turned out that the sheep were cannons painted white to camoflauge them from far away.

Burns lit a lantern so that the little rowboat could find their way back, which only gave the guns a new target. He quickly extinguished his lamp. But with the flash of the cannons, he now had a target for his big long range gun, which he used to great advantage. Deciding he had risked enough, he rowed out of the harbor with his sweeps. Once clear, having heard there were real sheep on the island, he sent his crew ashore to buy sheep, vegetables, and water. By sunup he was twenty miles away. He was only richer in terms of food and water. But he also had another daring story to share.

When deception would not work, guile was used. Guile, and violence. Burns was conniving and aggressive when dealing with British warships, but when he took the merchant ships, especially if they put up no fight, he was generally forgiving and graceful to his captors. When a group of British prisoners asked to be put ashore at a Spanish garrison, Burns at first hesitated. These Spanish colonial fortifications had little direct contact with Spain, and often operated by their own deceptive rules. They very well may not treat the British well.

It was a prediction that was all too accurate.

He sent a boat with one crew member and the British ashore, but it did not come back. When he sent a second boat with another crew member to find out what had happened, that one, too, did not return. The British and the two American sailors had all been thrown into prison. After much argument, the second boat and a single crewman was allowed to return with a message. The sailors would not be returned until the *Snap Dragon* anchored under the range of the fort's big guns.

Burns knew this was a ruse to take either his cargo or his ship, and refused. He dearly wanted his crew members back, but couldn't risk his ship and the rest of the sailors. Instead of acquiescing, he sailed off and waited for Spanish ships. He captured a Spanish felucca, took the passengers prisoner, and send the commander back with a simple message. Either return the boats with his crew in two hours or he would hang every member of the Spanish boat. He even tied nooses to his masts to resemble a gallows as he sailed back to the port.

The Spanish moved quickly to return the sailors to Burns and his ship. It turned out that the Spanish governor had his brother-in-law as one of the passengers.

His first cruise lasted more than six months and brought in prizes of over a million dollars, making both Burns and his crew not only highly successful, but more than moderately wealthy.

His second cruise would be even more profitable, with over $2.5 million in cargo and ships taken. Burns had also gotten something else. A reputation. He was quickly becoming an icon in the little ports of Beaufort and

Swansboro, and had become a bit of a hero to the rest of the American coast. He and his swift ship *Snap Dragon* had become somewhat infamous to the British. So much so that a man-o-war sent a message to Beaufort harbor calling him out for battle. The British schooner *Highflyer* challenged the *Snap Dragon* to a fight off of Cape Lookout. Burns promptly answered the challenge and sailed for the rendezvous point, but the British skipper and his ship were nowhere to be found. The *Highflyer* had taken the coward's way out, it seemed, because it was captured all of three days later far up in Nantucket.

For his second outing, Burns gained several British naval uniforms, so as to bluff his way close to merchant ships and to help acquire provisions. In order to avoid the heat of the summer, along with the added heat of threats from the British Navy in the Caribbean, he worked his way northward, where he chased down with ease several merchant ships even while they were under guard of armed vessels. He had found that the swift *Snap Dragon* could outrace any pursuers so quickly that he was able to take merchant ships, unload them of cargo, and then speed away before any naval frigates could chase him down.

After a month at sea, with provisions low, as the biggest risk to his crew was the lack of fresh and untainted water, he discovered a large fleet of British fishing vessels. He disguised both his ship and crew and went aboard several, exchanging fairly with the ships, rum for water. Some of the British captains had their doubts as to if the ship was actually British, but Burns treated them fairly, making honest deals with the fishermen, and never causing problems, so no one even bothered to say anything about the contact.

While his feats at sea were legendary, as he took prize after prize, what he did in port towns was equally as daring. After his encounter with the fishing fleet, he put in at a nearby fishing village. Having his men wear the same British uniforms, he spent well there, buying provisions and doing repairs. The locals were happy to have the ship there, as they brought much needed trade and money to the little port, and caused no problems among the townsfolk.

When he sailed out, he came upon the one ship that proved faster than he. A three masted schooner sailed in, almost passing head on, and Burns was not able to determine if the ship was a warship or trader until it had passed. The big schooner turned out to be of American design, carrying a load of valuable silk and other commodities, under a license of passage from Britain, an act greatly frowned upon by the Americans at war, as they were doing business with the enemy. The American craft proved too swift for even the *Snap Dragon*, and Burns cursed the day it got away.

When he couldn't take by force, or by conniving, or even through fair trade, Burns was still ingenious in his ability to find supplies. Being far to the north, Burns spied many icebergs floating from the Arctic in the cool summer around Labrador. He sent a boat to one, and discovered a fresh water lake on top, where his crew drained the cold fresh water into casks for his crew.

With so much success in such a small amount of time, after only two months, Burns had to return home. He had sent so many prize ships back with skeleton crews that he barely had enough men to run his own ship, along with the nearly one hundred prisoners he had aboard. Many were placed on prize ships with the honorable agreement that they were not to engage in war with the United States until they were "exchanged" with American prisoners. It was a dubious assumption, but it did rid Burns of some of the enormous supercargo of enemy passengers.

Though most were not the enemy to Burns. They were mostly other sailors and captains, equal in their effort, though less in skill, and Burns treated them fairly, often giving them the run of the deck instead of keeping them in irons. On his second return, before selling off the fine cloths and the large amount of skillfully manufactured tools, including sailmaking needles from Britain, Burns made sure that all captives could claim personal items from the collected treasure. Burns was licensed as a privateer, and saw himself as a commerce raider, but his fairness to others would never let him be a pirate. He only took from the country with which his was at war.

The second voyage would net him a much greater profit, and even the crews would take in over $3000, a hefty sum in 1812 for less than three month's work.

His third voyage would be his last. The profit he had made was too tempting to allow more voyages, and he was now a wealthy man. He had married in 1809, but his wife Joanna had left with his son to her family's home in New Bern right before his third voyage. Having rarely seen his son, and now losing his wife, who would soon pass away, may have also heeded the call to a life on land. Burns took his money and turned it into several businesses, including a shipbuilding firm in Swansboro, where he built the *Prometheus*, the first steamship in North Carolina, which cruised the Cape Fear. He lived in a stately home in Beaufort, and ran several businesses, including manufacturing bricks for the construction of Fort Macon and a salt works factory.

In 1821 he was elected to the North Carolina House of Commons, where he served seven terms, and then four terms in the NC Senate, representing Carteret County for fourteen years. His fairness in being a captain, even treating his captors well, would prove to be both his greatest strength and later his downfall. He was seen to be incredibly fair and honest in his political dealings, but to that end never took more for his county than he was willing to see taken from others in the state. When the western part of North Carolina began to grow in population, the larger eastern part had attempted to align the power in the state to greatly favor the eastern politicians and their districts. Burns thought that a more equitable voting right would be fair, and voted with the western representatives, giving them equal say in the state. The local voters, while still admiring the man, took umbrage and voted him out.

By then it was 1835, and Burns had lost much of his fortune. He had developed rheumatism from sailing from the heat of the Caribbean to the cold of the Arctic, and had little to fall back on. He was now sixty years old, remarried, with a young daughter. After his exit from North Carolina politics, the President of the United States stepped in. Andrew

Jackson, himself a veteran of the War of 1812, honored Burns with a simple appointment to the Brant Shoals Lifeboat. He would enjoy the simple life in the town of Portsmouth, tending to the light, while finding ample time to drink rum and argue with his neighbors. It was a fitting tribute to the great captain, and with it came an ample and continual payment. Burns would hold the position until he passed in 1850.

Burns was buried in Beaufort at the Anne Street Cemetery, next to the Methodist Church. This graveyard would become famous in later years as The Old Burying Ground, for its many famous interments and the age of the residents who rest there. When Otway Burns was laid to rest, he had long outlived his legend. He was just another old veteran, an old and cranky man who had seen his last day. He was buried without fanfare in the cemetery.

But others remembered his heroism, even if it took some time. The town of Burnsville, far off in the mountains of North Carolina, was named after the far flung sea captain from the coast. They honored the name of the man who spoke up for their equal rights as citizens of the state, and put up a monument to him in 1909.

But his greatest monument would remain with him. After his retirement from a life at sea, one of his guns from the *Snap Dragon* had been used as a demarcation line between the new and old sections of Beaufort. On July 24, 1901, Burns' grave was rededicated, with a new tomb, fittingly above ground for a sailor, and topped with the cannon from his beloved *Snap Dragon*.

As a sailor, captain, privateer, war hero, legend, politician, and even a lighthouse tender, Otway Burns served with a fairness and skill that has rarely been seen, before and since, but one which deserves the honor of a life well lived.

Afterword

I benefit from looking through the lens of history, without having to face it. I'll admit that right up front. What I wrote here is accurate, true to a point, and factual.

Now, how can we go about saying these things when a lot of these stories are obviously either created, imagined, or just made up? The same way we tell all our campfire stories. It's entertainment. As I once explained to a skeptical reader, "It's a ghost *story*." It's a tale, a bit of fantasy, a legend or history, and I tell it as such.

Did Blackbeard really think all the things I had him think? Of course I don't know, but I do know he wanted to go pirating and leave sleepy, boring Bath after less than a few months. And I doubt he was expecting to die in Ocracoke.

Is there really a fiery ship that burns but isn't consumed off of Ocracoke? Well... okay, probably not. But I tell ya, in my long life on the coast, I've seen stuff. I've seen the moon boil up out of the ocean all burning and orange, and if I didn't know it was coming, I would have thought it was a burning ship at sea. Having a fun, yes, fun, even though it was gory, tale to tell when that happens is like change in a little kid's pocket.

There is a lot of real history to these stories. Otway Burns really was this brash and daring captain. It's too bad we don't remember him more. The Nazi U-boats were more horrific than I even portray them. As Gramps said to Taffy Willis in *Taffy Of Torpedo Junction,* "These are bad toimes." And, no, I have no idea where Theodosia Burns met her end, whether it be in Nags Head or Bald Head.

But the stories are real. By that, I mean, we really have these stories we like to tell. Blackbeard's ghost story is as real as Blackbeard himself. Theodosia's portrait really exists, and it really was given to Dr. Poole. Christolph von Graffnreid was a real person who help found New Bern.

And I can tell you from personal experience that we had tar on our feet from walks on the beach, and I had a bottle of corn oil and paper towels in my family's garage, so I know those Nazi monsters sank hundreds of ship just off my coast.

The ghosts, the thoughts, the happenstance on a deck of a ship over three hundred years ago, well, I can only guess what was said and done. That's my job, see, to paint the story with words to put you, my dear reader, there, right in the salt spray and burning black powder, as best as I can.

I'll leave the job of telling the dull, correct, and narrow parts of history to someone else.

And if you are here at the end of the book, you at least like my stories as much as the clinical stuff that someone else can write.

So, yes, there is a lot more to each story in this book. If I wanted to, I could have made it a bit longer, and you probably wouldn't be at the end yet.

Which leads me to one other interesting subject I discovered. And discovered is the right word.

This is maybe a continuation of my ghost stories, albeit in

pirate form. I originally considered doing the same thirteen lucky tales I did in those other books. But I thought I could do more. Then I discovered that there really weren't a lot of the classical pirates that existed along North Carolina's coast at the turn of the 1700s. There's a good reason why we love Blackbeard so much. He's about all we got.

Though I would strenuously argue for wood figures of both Otway Burns and Horatio Sinbad in our gift shops, equally deserving of honors and notoriety.

So, with a bit of work, and some stories I already knew, I gathered up a few more pirates. I had written about Captain Kidd in my first book, *Did You See That?* so I knew that story well. And, yes, Stede Bonnet did spend some time on our coast. But I had to find some more, and it was really interesting to find the little tales, and the bigger histories that we don't tell when someone is always trying to explain how we got Blackbeard wrong. I had no idea how prevalent the Spanish pirates were on our coast, nor knew how bloodthirsty and ruthless they were.

So, well, I guess I learned a little something with this book, and I made it fun while doing it.

Now, go ahead, finish up, then put on the puffy shirt and long black coat, and go put yer knee up on something. We all want to be pirates. Don't let anything get in your way.

Here's to you, you pirates, rogues, saboteurs, and rascals. I give you the better half of the great pirate Benjamin Hornigold's toast, "Here's to a merry life!"

Joe Sledge

About The Author

Joe Sledge is the author of, oh, let me count now, eleven books. Really, that many, huh? As well as publisher and editor of several republished Outer Banks books.

Joe grew up in an un-air conditioned beach house in Kill Devil Hills when he was a little boy. The youngest of four sons to his parents, he was often put on the sofa with a chair next to it to keep him from falling off. But that was okay, because he got to wander off to the sun deck at night in hopes of seeing ghost pirates sail in to dig up buried treasure that was salted away hundreds of years ago. That bit of imagination has led to a love of pirates and lore on the Outer Banks to this day.

Joe graduated from the University of North Carolina, where he once, at least once, dressed up as a pirate with a costume he made with his mom's help (thanks, Mom!) on Franklin Street for Halloween.

Joe is happily married with a daughter. He still has his father's little Boston Whaler sailboat, which he hopes to fix up one day, if he ever sells enough books. It may not get him out to sea, but he's still good at playing pirate.

Image Credits

All images by Joe Sledge unless otherwise noted. No images may be reproduced without written permission from the owner.

Captain Kidd drawing - public domain
Captain Horatio Sinbad and *Meka* II - courtesy Horatio Sinbad
Simon Fernando ship - John White drawings, public domain
Azores harbor - public domain
Carroll A. Deering - public domain
Carroll A. Deering at sea -Thomas Jacobson, U.S. government image, public domain.
Carroll A. Deering wreck - public domain
Hewitt postcard - public domain
Theodosia Burr portrait - public domain
Stede Bonnet etching - public domain
Flaming Ship of Ocracoke - public domain
U-boat attack - U.S. government image, public domain
V-boat - U.S. government image, public domain
Otway Burns portrait -public domain
Burns grave - Walter Francis Burns, public domain